1. In the Silence of Solitude

IN THE SILENCE OF SOLITUDE

"Blessed is he who possesses Bethlehem in his heart,
and in whose heart Christ is born daily.
For what is the meaning of Bethlehem if not
"House of Bread"? Let us, too, become a house of bread
which came down from heaven."

St. Jerome (c. 340-420) who lived as a hermit
in Bethlehem near the Judean Desert

In the Silence of Solitude

Contemporary Witnesses of the Desert

Compiled and Edited by Eugene Romano, HBHJ
Desert Father

ALBA·HOUSE   NEW·YORK

SOCIETY OF ST. PAUL, 2187 VICTORY BLVD., STATEN ISLAND, NEW YORK 10314

Library of Congress Cataloging-in-Publication Data

In the silence of solitude: contemporary witnesses of the desert /
    compiled and edited by Eugene Romano.
        p.   cm.
    ISBN 0-8189-0754-1
    1. Hermits of Bethlehem of the Heart of Jesus — Spiritual life.
    2. Solitude — Religious aspects — Catholic Church. 3. Desert Fathers.
    4. Deserts — Religious aspects — Christianity. 5. Wilderness
    (Theology) 6. Spirituality — Catholic Church. 7. Catholic Church —
    Doctrines.   I. Romano, Eugene L.
    BX3674.5.I6   1995
    255'.79 — dc20   95-42971
                                                          CIP

Produced and designed in the United States of America by the
Fathers and Brothers of the Society of St. Paul,
2187 Victory Boulevard, Staten Island, New York 10314,
as part of their communications apostolate.

ISBN: 0-8189-0754-1

Printing Information:

Current Printing - first digit	1	2	3	4	5	6	7	8	9	10

Year of Current Printing - first year shown

1995	1996	1997	1998	1999	2000

Dedication

This work is fondly dedicated
with much gratitude to
Bishop Frank J. Rodimer, D.D.,
Ordinary of the Diocese of Paterson,
for his confidence and support,
and to
Bishop Lawrence B. Casey, D.D.
of happy memory,
both of whom have made possible
the "hermitage experience"
at Bethlehem
for all the pilgrims who have given witness
within these pages.

Table of Contents

Foreword

Have you ever had a spiritual director? Do you know what spiritual direction is? Perhaps I can explain it best by first telling you what it is not. It is not therapeutic counselling, although guidance might be useful when needed. A parent-child relationship is not the goal of spiritual direction. Spiritual direction is not teaching, although enlightened information may be given by the director from time to time.

The role of the spiritual director is primarily one of listening, clarifying, and discerning. Spiritual direction is a one-to-one relationship for the purpose of fostering spiritual growth and encouragement.

Clarification aims at helping the directee to grow in self-knowledge. Questions are proposed: Are you a person of faith? Do you have enough confidence to trust the Lord in all circumstances? Do you love others cheerfully and generously? The object of this inquiry involves your level of faith, hope and charity, that is, the theological virtues.

Discernment is a more specialized gift. It focuses on the hidden mystery of the Holy Spirit, who leads us along paths we would not have chosen for ourselves. "What is God asking of you at this time in your life?"

A good director never plays God. You must discover God's will for yourself through prayerful reflection. Answers may flow out of a mutually cooperative dialogue, but the directee is never allowed to become dependent on the director. Both parties have to work toward the same goal, namely, spiritual maturity.

What you are about to read is a book of wisdom compiled and edited by a gifted spiritual director. Father Gene Romano is what I would call a contemporary Desert Father, a modern day hermit. He has devoted his entire priestly life, about 40 years at this writing, to living the Gospel in a unique way, loving God generously and wholeheartedly in a ministry of silence and solitude. By doing this he has learned to live joyfully in the embrace of God's love.

I have known Father Romano since 1956 when I entered the Seminary of the Immaculate Conception which at the time was located in Darlington, New Jersey. We both studied for the Diocese of Paterson. After ordination we both worked in parish ministry. Eventually, I became the clergy personnel director, and Gene became the pastor of Our Lady of Pompei Parish in Paterson.

One day he came to speak to me about his desire to enter more deeply into a life of contemplative prayer. This yearning began years before in the seminary. I remember a conversation I had with him back in 1958. It was about Blessed Elizabeth of the Trinity, a contemplative nun and mystic who wrote: "Heaven is God, and since God is in us, our heaven has already begun." She opened his eyes to the power of the indwelling Trinity.

Knowing the depth of his conviction about his new calling, I recommended to Bishop Lawrence Casey that he allow Father Romano to dedicate himself exclusively to prayer. Because he understood this special vocation, Bishop Casey agreed to let him go. That was 25 years ago. He released Father Romano to create the Bethlehem Hermitage, which has become a spiritual haven for many hundreds of searchers, several of whom have contributed their own personal testimony to this book which is the fruit of his and their prayerful dedication to seeking the will of God and the holiness to which He calls us all.

Even though you may not be called to live in prayerful isolation — most of those whose testimony is recorded here were not, you are still called to holiness. May the Lord bless and protect you, and may He be your strength and your joy as you savor each brief section of this book and experience for yourself God's love pouring out of every page. Along with Father Romano, my prayer is that, in the process, it will help you to grow closer to God as well.

Rev. John Catoir, JCD
Director Emeritus of *The Christophers*
President of *St. Jude Media Ministry*

Introduction

"So I will allure them; I will lead them into the desert and speak to their hearts." Hosea 2:16

"He led His people across the desert, for His love is everlasting." Psalm 136:16

Since the beginning, God has been calling His people to *new life*, and inviting them into the *land of changes*. It is a silent land full of shadows, darkness and insecurities. Abraham and Sarah started their great journey after hearing His call to the pristine wilderness of the desert, a land of mystery where unquestionable faith and reverence are necessary.

Moses passed through the desert in search of the promised land while trying to lead God's people from slavery into the freedom of Yahweh's life as His chosen people. But because of their stony hearts and refusal to surrender completely to the Father's call, they were blinded to the many-splendored beauty on the divine horizon.

John the Baptist, that proto-hermit of the New Testament and solitary soul in perfect surrender to the divine will, went into the desert to become a voice *crying in the wilderness* for straight paths to the Lord. These great figures left what they knew, their everyday and habitual reactions to experience, and took on a *new mind*. They crossed a desert, took a step toward God, were turned around — converted — experienced a *pass-over* and a new freedom. Their invitation is shared by all believers.

Even the weakest has strength enough through the power won by the great Witness and High Priest, Jesus Christ, to respond to the call to a *new life* and a *new mind* which gives greater communion with the

Church, the Mystical Body of Christ, and with all the saints — past, present and to come. Solitude expands the freedom to respond to the Spirit within, crying out for the fullness of the promised Kingdom.

Jesus' predilection for solitary prayer and desert retreat as a source of spiritual energy is repeated over and over again in the Gospels. Opening His public ministry with a journey into the desert for an encounter with the Devil (or the spirits of evil), the Son of God often returns to the desert to be alone in prayer and to receive strength to continue His life of teaching and preaching the good news of salvation for all.

Alone with God in the desert wasteland and aware of His oneness with the Father, Jesus experiences the explosive love that will ultimately give Him strength enough to hang on the *desert* of His Cross. In the solitude of the Cross — in abandonment and pain — Christ redeemed the world. Only when He appeared to humankind as a worthless, helpless *no-thing*, a *worm and no man*, in complete surrender to His Father's will and reduced to sin itself could He complete the redemptive act — for all humankind.

On the Cross, Jesus appeared to have lost His humanity, wrung from Him drop by drop, even abandoned by the One Whose will He came to do. To the passers-by He was a shocking exhibit of foolishness, a man to be jeered at and ridiculed. "Others he saved, himself he cannot save" (Mk 15:31). But it was in this nothingness that He perfectly fulfilled His Father's will for Him. Why?

The mysteries of the Cross and the desert are bound together with the same answer. The voice in His heart that sustained Jesus on the Cross is as exclusive to its listener as the voice that leads those who will hear into the desert to be ego-reduced and purified of the false self. Stripping the self of pretension can be as uncomfortable and blistering as a walk on hot, burning sand, but it is the only pathway into the sanctuary of one's soul where the Divine Guide waits to enfold the traveler in the mysterious embrace of the Trinity. The journey begins when we strain to hear, over the clamorous and beguiling attractions of the world, the gentle voice of God in the center of our hearts.

It is in the desert emptiness, the hushed silence, that God whispers to our yearning hearts as he did to Abraham: "Leave your native land and your ancestral home for the country which I will show you" (Gn 12:1-4). The desert becomes a journey of the soul in faith as God intently pursues His chosen people. It is a call and a response to love. "Understand, then, that the Lord, your God, is God indeed, the faithful God Who keeps His merciful covenant towards those who love Him and keep His commandments" (Dt 7:6-11).

Third-century Christian hermits listened for the *voice of God* in the clear, silent air of the Egyptian and Judean deserts. They became the earliest models of solitary prayer and desert spirituality within the Christian Church. That model lives on in the present as communities of modern cenobites and/or hermits strive for a life of unceasing prayer and silent listening for the word of God in Scripture in the midst of a noisy world.

These hermits and monastics are not yet saints but are ordinary believers who are trying to answer the challenge of the question asked by all Christians: *"What more must I do to have eternal life?"* (Mt 19:16). It is to the Laura called the Hermits of Bethlehem in the Heart of Jesus in Chester, New Jersey, that I wish to introduce you.

Through the clamor of a very active and happy ministry as a diocesan parish priest, I discerned a clear calling to pursue a more solitary, prayerful and faith-dependent way of life where the usual markers were absent. My Bishop encouraged my call but warned of the hardships I would surely encounter in founding a Laura of Hermits. Twenty years later the Hermits of Bethlehem in the Heart of Jesus are a reality.

The call to the kind of life we are attempting to lead is extraordinary within the universal Church. Since it is God Who asks — and simply because He asks — it is reason enough for the hermit to say "Yes." We are an eremitical, contemplative public association of Catholic men and women approved and erected by the Bishop of the Diocese of Paterson and under his ecclesiastical authority. Our striving for ever more intimate union with God's will for His people is supported by our association together as solitaries. Each hermit lives in obedience to the Desert Father* who, in imitation of Jesus, ministers to the brothers and sisters by leadership.

Based upon the Gospel of Jesus Christ, hermit spirituality reflects the spirit and teachings of the Desert Fathers and Mothers of the early Church. Its response within the Church is to a call to unceasing prayer, penance and solitude of heart and mind for the praise of God and for the salvation of the world as God wills the world saved (Canon 603).

The Hermits of Bethlehem live in separate, solitary hermitages around a chapel and central house. United to one another and to all in the Heart of Jesus, each one's life in hermitage is a visible expression of his availability to encounter God, as God chooses to reveal Himself through Scripture and Sacrament, so as to be continually transformed into the likeness of Christ.

The *real desert wilderness experience* takes place within the heart. Like Jesus in solitary prayer, the hermit is led into this desert by the Holy Spirit. The hermit surrenders continually to the Father, yields with Jesus to the Father's will, depends on God alone for everything and listens to the Spirit within us whispering "Abba, Father." Like Jesus, the hermit longs to become rooted in a divinized love, a selfless love that rises from the ashes of a sacrificial life and becomes a fragrant incense ascending before the Face of God. Unlike Jesus, the hermit is in a constant state of conversion to faith, hope and love. His transformation is possible only because Jesus is loved by the Father Who, for the sake of His Son, loves each one. Jesus' sacrificial love for our sakes "does not come to an end" (1 Cor 13:8).

St. Paul's words are ever before us: "I fill up what is lacking in the suffering of Christ for the sake of His Body, the Church" (Col 1:24). Through fidelity to the hidden life, the hermit's prayer becomes outstretched arms, imploring the Father by the Spirit's power that His will be done in the lives of all brothers and sisters. Evagrius Ponticus

---

* Whenever the masculine is used, the feminine can be substituted, e.g., Desert Father/Mother, his/her, etc.

believed "a monk is someone who is separated from everything and united to everybody." The hermit life witnesses to the words of St. John of the Cross: "The slightest movement of pure love is more useful to the Church than all other works together."

The hermit's participation in this great mystery is not an occasion of *pride*. Rather, he is made humble in realizing how far he is from *the movements of pure love*. Like all people of God, each hermit has experienced in his personal life pain and suffering, joy and consolation, emptiness and tears. Through a communion of suffering and living with the entire People of God, the hermit daily becomes a more compassionate lover of God, oneself, and all of God's broken children.

The passover from death to resurrection that we all desire with Jesus requires "that the grain of wheat die," so that we no longer remain alone. "For there is no greater love than that one lay down his life for his friends" (Jn 15:13). The hermit strives, therefore, to be a living Bethlehem, literally a House of Bread, handing his prayers over to the Father that the whole world might eat of His will.

Daniel Walsh, Thomas Merton's lifelong mentor, found a relationship between prayer and service: "Most are called to salvation primarily through witnessing to God in man by loving service to others. The contemplative . . . finds salvation primarily through witnessing to man in God by a life of fidelity to contemplative prayer."

Fully aware of his brothers' and sisters' pain, the hermit dies for them on the cross of solitude and, like Christ, becomes most powerful in death to himself for the other. "In our body we always carry Jesus' death, so that in our body Jesus' life may also be seen" (2 Cor 4:10). How inspiring to read:

"Active works are essential, but their effort is particular and limited. One who realistically wishes to do something for the world and the human race on a large scale might best devote oneself to a life of prayer, obedience, penance, solitude, and silence. That is how the Church has always embarked on "renewal." That is how the great efforts launched by the saints started, as witness the hermits of the Thebaid, Benedict at Subiaco, Francis at La Verna, Ignatius at Manresa, Teresa of Jesus, and many more. Jesus Himself fasted in the desert.

Whenever there has been in the Church what subsequent generations have recognized as a major renewal, it has started with individuals or small groups who have cared enough to go out into the desert or to the hermitage or to the cloister to wrestle alone with God and Satan, in the solitude of contemplative prayer" (*The Teaching of Christ*, Lawler, Wuerl and Lawler, eds. Our Sunday Visitor Books, 1976, 1995 (4th ed.) p. 321).

That the hermit's immersion in silence and solitude effects a dynamic union with all in God is difficult for moderns to accept and practice. The fabled American *work ethic* has fashioned an activist people conditioned from childhood to *do*. Unless we are *doing*, we are considered worthless and even selfish, utterly lacking in responsibility: *Idle hands are the Devil's workshop*. The young and impressionable often suffer guilt and confusion when their spiritual selves are being formed by the Spirit to be contemplatives while they are being conditioned by their environment to be *doers*.

Within the womb of silence and solitude, the spiritual being and true self of the Hermit of Bethlehem is continually being formed (Ps 139:13). United with all created beings, responsible for them in one's prayer, one's silence in speech and thought speaks to God of Himself and others, and of God to others. Far from being special or extraordinary, the hermit is called to live out the life in ordinariness for reasons known only to God. Deep within the hermit's being is given a *fiat*, an assent to let God have His way.

God's ways have always been preposterous and foolish to the logical. Of Jesus it was said, "He is out of his mind" (Mk 3:31). To the pragmatic and worldly the hermit's life can seem downright wasteful, even selfish. Aware of contemporary thinking, the Hermit of Bethlehem yet answers the Master's call and keeps his eyes on Jesus, while striving to be a living Bethlehem — a House of Bread. This life of solitude is given entirely to the love of God and to Him alone for His own sake.

In contemplation the hermit waits upon God. He enters solitude with an intense yearning for Him and is led alone by God on a unique and private journey, responding to Him in secret. This is a hidden and private conversation of love with the Lord so that the word is made flesh in each hermit (cf. Jn 1:14). In the silence of speech and thought the hermit speaks most truly with God in contemplation, waiting for the interior voice of the Lord Who will "give to him hidden treasures and the concealed riches of secret places" (Is 45:3).

Prayer is the bread of the hermit's life. It is living in the mystery of God Who dwells in the depths of one's being and Whom one finds in every event and circumstance of one's life and, more deeply, in one another. Though solitary, the hermit does not live in isolation, but in communion with and humbly making intercession for the Body of Christ, real and mystical. The Liturgy of the Hours, the prayer of the Church, is a school of continual prayer and an integral part of the hermit's life. The hermit, a heartbeat in the Church, is conscious of Christ praying the Hours with and in him. For the hermit, prayer is not a religious exercise, it is one's life orientation, the breath of one's soul.

The Sacred Scriptures are the lungs of the hermit's daily prayer — he does not live without them. Reading, pondering and praying the Scriptures becomes the Bread of the Word, complementing the nourishment one receives from the Bread of the Eucharist. "Not on bread alone does man live but on every word that comes from the mouth of God" (Mt 4:4). "If you live according to My word, you are truly My disciples; then you will know the truth and the truth will set you free" (Jn 8:31-32).

The Eucharistic Sacrifice is the heart of the hermit's day. The Holy Eucharist is the food for a life of prayer and a channel to God's Trinitarian life. The Eucharist is the *new Manna* sustaining the hermit in a desert journey that imitates the progress of the Israelites through the desert to the Promised Land. Eucharistic adoration is central to life in the desert. Living hidden in the Eucharistic Heart of Jesus, in the presence of the Father, one's Eucharistic prayer pervades all of life, work, conscious and unconscious moments, so that with Jesus, the hermit is bread for the brothers and sisters, and for the life of the whole world.

After Jesus, Mary, Mother of the Church, Woman of Faith, Queen of the Desert is the patroness and exemplar of the eremitical vocation. Like Mary, the hermit strives to be a servant-bearer of the Word. Like her and the saints, one remains open to God and surrenders himself in trust that the day to day experience is the mysterious revelation of His plan. We turn to Mary by her Son's special invitation from the Cross: "Woman, behold your son. Son, behold your mother" (Jn 19:26, 27).

Mary's selfless surrender to the Father inspires and strengthens the Hermit of Bethlehem in his will to abandon oneself on the spiritual journey toward the Blessed Trinity. The hermit joins Mary in seeing and embracing God in every event and moment, thus becoming a living Bethlehem, loving others by being lost in the Love of God. Mary's Magnificat of praise and love becomes the hermit's program of life as he strives to be poor in spirit, to be little and humble and always to live in the hope and joy of the Gospel of Jesus.

The Hermit of Bethlehem strives to live in the spirit of the Beatitudes: to be poor in spirit, to be a peacemaker, to mourn with those who mourn, to seek justice on earth. Living in a state of continual conversion to the conviction that God loves us, forgives us, welcomes us back and recreates us in His love, the Hermit of Bethlehem is aware of the needs of others and is always "clothing himself with heartfelt mercy, with kindness, humility, meekness and patience" (Col 3:12). Through the faithful and joyful living of the vows of poverty, chastity and obedience, the hermit centers his life on God as each one responds to Him in prayer, sacrifice and labor for the Church of Christ. "The life I live is not my own; Christ is living in me" (Gal 2:20).

The Canon Law of the Church recognizes hermits as dedicated to God in consecrated life when they publicly profess, by vow or some other sacred bond, the three evangelical counsels and lead their particular form of life under the guidance of the diocesan bishop. Canon 603: "Beside institutes of consecrated life, the Church recognizes the life of hermits or anchorites, in which Christ's faithful withdraw further from the world and devote their lives to the praise of God and the salvation of the world in the *silence of solitude* and through constant prayer and penance."

The hermit's perseverance in this wholly dedicated life provides the power that converts and transforms the Body of Christ, the Church. This life is an extension of Christ's own desert prayer. It is united to Him in His Mystical Body, living through the Holy Spirit and bringing the Church to the Father. As a son of the Church, the Hermit of Bethlehem pledges loyalty and obedience to the Holy Father, the Vicar of Christ on earth, to the magisterium of the Church and to the Ordinary, the Bishop of Paterson. He fondly embraces the inspired words of Scripture: "Obey your leaders and submit to them, for they keep watch over you as men who must render an account. So act that they may fulfill their task with joy, not with sorrow" (Heb 13:17).

Finally, the hermit lives only for the Love that began with the birth of Jesus in the manger at Bethlehem and grew through His death on the Cross and Resurrection into His Mystical Body. He strives to be a living House of Bread, rooted in Jesus, the Living Bread come down from heaven. His Love must radiate in each one's life, especially in the way guests are received. The Eucharistic and Scriptural Bread by which the hermit lives becomes the Bread of Hospitality, a quality of the heart which depends not on what I do for someone, but who I am for someone.

The Hermits of Bethlehem welcome clergy, religious and laity into our desert to share our solitude and silence. Our Desert Hospitality is a quality of welcoming and a silent presence. We prefer an atmosphere of prayer to a program of prayer for our guests. Our Desert Hospitality helps to create this atmosphere, especially for priests who are called to feed the People of God. As the shepherds and the Magi were drawn to the manger of the Nativity, Bethlehem Hermitage is a presence in the Church drawing to itself all who would come for healing and renewal and to offer silent homage to our Lord and Savior.

Many have accepted the hospitality of our Laura in Chester, New Jersey since we welcomed our first guests. Some have offered written, moving testimony of their experiences at Bethlehem, and what follows is a sample of their witness to the effects of days or weeks spent with us in solitude and prayer. It is the Holy Spirit who has acted upon them — it is nothing we hermits have of ourselves — and for this action of grace we praise God.

You, too, who read this are invited to Bethlehem. Come into our solitude and eat of the Word and Sacrament of the Lord with an intensity that will reward you with special possibilities for healing and renewal.

After Eucharistic Adoration each day, the Hermit of Bethlehem prays the Bethlehem Prayer for entry into the Triune Mystery of Love. He implores the Community of Three in One to permeate his life, the lives of the guests, and creation everywhere, so that with Jesus all might become Bread, Bread for one another and for the whole world.

To you who read this each Hermit of Bethlehem sends blessings for your peace and for faith for your journey.

Eugene Romano, Desert Father
Hermits of Bethlehem
in the Heart of Jesus
Chester, New Jersey
Christmas, 1995

Notes

In citing works in the notes, short titles have generally been used. Works frequently cited have been identified by the following abbreviations:

DC   Benedicta Ward, *The Desert Christian: the Sayings of the Desert Fathers* (New York: Macmillan Publishing Co., Inc., 1975)

DRDF   Benedicta Ward, *Daily Readings with the Desert Fathers* (Springfield: Templegate Publishers, 1988)

DW   Yushi Nomura, *Desert Wisdom: Sayings from the Desert Fathers* (London: Cistercian Publications, 1980)

LOVE   Bishop Chrysostomos, *Love: A Fourth and Last Volume in the Series "Themes in Orthodox Patristic Psychology"* (Brookline: Holy Cross Orthodox Press, 1990)

SB   Anthony de Mello, *The Song of the Bird* (Garden City: Image Books, 1984)

SDF   Benedicta Ward, *The Sayings of the Desert Fathers* (Kalamazoo: Cistercian Publications, 1984)

TWD   Douglas Burton-Christie, *The Word in the Desert: Scripture and the Quest for Holiness in Early Christian Monasticism* (New York: Oxford University Press, 1993)

WA   Owen Chadwick, *Western Asceticism* (Philadelphia: The Westminster Press, 1963)

WD   Thomas Merton, *The Wisdom of the Desert: Sayings from the Desert Fathers of the Fourth Century* (New York: New Directions, 1970)

WDF   Benedicta Ward, *The Wisdom of the Desert Fathers: Systematic Sayings from the Anonymous Series of the Apophthegmata Patrum* (Oxford: SLG Press, 1986)

Biblical Abbreviations

OLD TESTAMENT

Genesis	Gn	Nehemiah	Ne	Baruch	Ba
Exodus	Ex	Tobit	Tb	Ezekiel	Ezk
Leviticus	Lv	Judith	Jdt	Daniel	Dn
Numbers	Nb	Esther	Est	Hosea	Ho
Deuteronomy	Dt	1 Maccabees	1 M	Joel	Jl
Joshua	Jos	2 Maccabees	2 M	Amos	Am
Judges	Jg	Job	Jb	Obadiah	Ob
Ruth	Rt	Psalms	Ps	Jonah	Jon
1 Samuel	1 S	Proverbs	Pr	Micah	Mi
2 Samuel	2 S	Ecclesiastes	Ec	Nahum	Na
1 Kings	1 K	Song of Songs	Sg	Habakkuk	Hab
2 Kings	2 K	Wisdom	Ws	Zephaniah	Zp
1 Chronicles	1 Ch	Sirach	Si	Haggai	Hg
2 Chronicles	2 Ch	Isaiah	Is	Malachi	Ml
Ezra	Ezr	Jeremiah	Jr	Zechariah	Zc
		Lamentations	Lm		

NEW TESTAMENT

Matthew	Mt	Ephesians	Eph	Hebrews	Heb
Mark	Mk	Philippians	Ph	James	Jm
Luke	Lk	Colossians	Col	1 Peter	1 P
John	Jn	1 Thessalonians	1 Th	2 Peter	2 P
Acts	Ac	2 Thessalonians	2 Th	1 John	1 Jn
Romans	Rm	1 Timothy	1 Tm	2 John	2 Jn
1 Corinthians	1 Cor	2 Timothy	2 Tm	3 John	3 Jn
2 Corinthians	2 Cor	Titus	Tt	Jude	Jude
Galatians	Gal	Philemon	Phm	Revelation	Rv

IN THE SILENCE OF SOLITUDE

The Fullness of Joy in God's Presence

"In God alone is my soul at rest" (Ps 62:1). God's presence is my supreme joy and happiness! The solitude and silence of this hermitage which enables and makes possible for me to tend towards the goal of full awareness of God's presence drew me to become a Hermit of Bethlehem. What more can I desire than being in an atmosphere conducive to daily striving for a total consciousness of God, keeping a loving gaze on the Beloved and living under His loving gaze, allowing His Person and the Gospel to take on life and depth in me?

Just being in His presence, listening with a receptive and attentive heart or simply telling Him of my love over and over is my joy. "That My own joy may be in you and your joy may be complete" (Jn 15:11).

I am also fully conscious of my humanity and daily shortcomings. These areas within me are still in need of conversion. All of these keep me humble, reminding me of my nothingness and dependence on God. Relying on His strength and trusting in Him, I experience His acceptance, love and peace. Reflecting on how much God has forgiven me, shown His love for me, and taken care of me overwhelms me with much gratitude and joy.

> *Abba Amoun of Nitria came to see Abba Anthony and said to him, "Since my rule is stricter than yours, how is it that your name is better known amongst men than mine is?" Abba Anthony answered, "It is because I love God more than you."* (SDF, p. 31, #1)

God's call from my former contemplative community to the desert of Bethlehem Hermitage is the highlight of my life. My *impossible dream* of many years, my yearning for the precious solitude and silence, which dispose me for a more intimate union with the Heart of Jesus in the Triune God in more intensive love, adoration and praise, has materialized. As much as is humanly possible on this earth, this hermitage creates the place where no other thought, no other interest than God takes place — to the extent we respond to God's grace and our humanity allows. This is the fullness of joy in His presence.

To keep alive the fire of love, I recall one or another of my favorite Scripture passages. These help me to live in the love and awareness of God. Saying the passage slowly, allowing it to be absorbed in me, savoring and reflecting on it, redirect me to a more intense recollection, until the words are no longer necessary. A few of these Scripture texts are:

"Set me like a seal on Your heart" (Sg 8:6).
"In God alone is my soul at rest" (Ps 62:1).
"You will show me the path of life, fullness of joys in
   Your presence" (Ps 16:11).
"I have loved you with an everlasting love" (Jr 31:3).
"Of You my heart has spoken: 'Seek His face.' It is
   Your face, O Lord, that I seek" (Ps 27:8).
"I love You, Lord, my strength, my rock, my fortress,
   my savior, my shield, my mighty help, my stronghold"
   (Ps 18:1-3).
"Like the deer that yearns for running streams, so my
   soul is yearning for You, my God" (Ps 42:2).
"My soul is thirsting for God, the God of my life; when
   can I enter and see the face of God" (Ps 42:3).

Hermit of Bethlehem

An old man said, "The monk's cell is like the furnace of Babylon where the three children found the Son of God, and it is like the pillar of cloud where God spoke with Moses." (WDF, p. 24, #74)

At Home with the Living Christ

Bethlehem Hermitage is a holy birthplace where the fullness of Christ can be received in new ways. It truly is a place where Jesus can *speak to your heart.* Because of the space created, I had the grace to *see* treasures that I probably run over daily. Through God's word, a gesture, the sacraments, a stone, a thistle, a station, a mourning dove, labor, laughter, refreshments all became signposts carved for my walk with the Lord.

It is a home where Christ has the freedom to serve us in a profoundly intimate way through His overwhelming love and through the generous selflessness of those who live there and love Him. I always will be grateful.

> *Abba Anthony said, "I no longer fear God, but I love Him. For love casts out fear."*
> (SDF, p. 8, #32)

I believe the hermitage calls us *away* to find a home and be at home with the living Christ. We are beautifully bombarded both silently and evidently with a holy lifestyle that centers on Jesus. It seems to invite us into a longing to make that *home* happen where we are. That can be frustrating for most of us. Believing that Jesus is so in love with us that He wants to and does *make His home in us* is a lifelong reminder and a challenge.

Bethlehem witnesses not only to the possibility, but the hope. It plants the seeds. It says: "Seek first the Kingdom of God" in all ways. Call upon Him, turn to Him, return to Him. Make space, clean house, simplify. Be transformed in His image. Forgive. First things first.

The profound stillness of the hermitage teaches us how to *listen* with our hearts. In and out of season, the Lord is with us. Give us the grace to say *yes* each day to You.

Laywoman, Wife and Mother

3

"Here's to Us"

Early in our formation, as we began to learn about meditation, we were told to get ourselves a "composition of place" — which means "Put yourself in the scene. What was it like?" When two of the apostles met Jesus for the first time, they asked Him, "Where do you live?" He responded, "Come and see." In meditating on that scene, my mind's eye took me to a small cabin in the woods, exactly down to every detail like the one I was standing in front of, here at Bethlehem Hermitage! I knew then that Jesus had *called* me to this spot, and my weekend progressed accordingly.

The next morning as I took the Chalice into my hands to receive Jesus in the Eucharist, the words, "Here's to us" transfixed themselves in my mind. Strange words, strange experience, yet I pondered them for the rest of the day. I tried to find some comparison to *US-ness*. Lord, it's not just YOU — *and* me. It's US together as one unit. It's Your Divine Indwelling in every part of me.

Abba Lot went to see Abba Joseph and said to him, "Abba, as far as I can, I say my little Office, I fast a little, I pray and meditate, I live in peace and, as far as I can, I purify my thoughts. What else can I do?" Then the old man stood up and stretched his hands towards heaven. His fingers became like ten lamps of fire and he said to him, "If you will, you can become all flame." (SDF, p. 103, #7)

It's like I'm an empty glove and You're the hand that has the power to control my every movement.

It's like I'm the encasement on a seed, or on a grain of wheat — and You are the Life within.

It's like 'E.T.' — and You have turned on Your heart light.

Maybe it's like all of these — maybe it's like none of these. I'm not sure. All I know is that You live in me, and You love in me, and You love through me. This call by God to come away with Him for the

4

weekend has deepened my spiritual life. That was eleven years ago, and I still return each year — not to *find God*, but rather to *be found* by Him.

I go to my ministry each day to be His Healing Presence to our broken world. A poor simple vessel filled with the love of God, to be poured out each day.

My prayer for you who read this today is that you, too, will "Come and see."

Sister of St. Joseph of Chestnut Hill

The Cross: Symbol of Love
for God and Love for Neighbor

Because I need to spend time alone with my God, I set apart one week to vacation with Him to be spiritually re-created. Jesus freely gifts and personally calls me to spend this precious time with Him — just the two of us — to lose myself in Him. I am on holy fire to arrive at my desert oasis to again be refreshed in Jesus. Here I am, Lord. I thank and praise You for this privileged experience. I empty and detach myself of the crowded, noisy, busy world; and, in complete faith and trust, I let God take control. In the silence and solitude of my heart, Jesus — *the Way, the Truth and the Life* — speaks and teaches me, showing me how to live in the world by putting my life in perspective, positioning Him first in my life. I do not come to the hermitage to escape the world, but to find a deeper union with my God — I in Him, He in me. The divine increasing, the human decreasing. Transforming — conforming — me to His image and likeness, becoming rooted and centered in Him, being nourished with the Bread of Life. The stillness and quiet — with no distractions — is conducive to concentrating on the interior presence of God. God uses the hermitage for my spiritual disciplining, making my whole life and lifestyle a prayer. Alone with the Alone in gifted contemplation, I come to know and to love the blessed name of Mary, singing my own Magnificat. As a result of this desert experi-

5

ence, my interior union with my God becomes a bridge to my outward expression of love to others. The perpendicular line of the cross is love for my God — the horizontal line is that same love for my neighbor. They cannot be separated!

Not taking my God for granted, I continually work at our relationship by these learned disciplines:

Reciting the Rosary daily, honoring our Lady
Celebrating daily Mass — listening and reflecting on the Word.
Ministering and serving all in an unconditional, gentle, forgiving love relationship.
Involvement in community.
Turning to God daily, raising my mind to Him, ever praising and thanking Him.
Enjoying each everyday, ordinary act without thinking ahead to the next.
Submitting and giving in to others — not needing to control and have my own way.
Seeing the beauty and dignity within — recognizing each person as another Christ.

Laywoman, Mother, Wife and Teacher

Letting God Love Me

If I were to try and express in a few words my stay at the hermitage, I would say quite simply that it was a time for doing nothing other than letting God love me. Through my openness to God's love I was in touch virtually with every part of creation and especially every human person created and loved by Him. I was there for no other reason.

It was a time for stopping my regular activity to focus all my attention and all my energies on God's loving presence and to open my whole being to His invitation to *make your home with Me.*

Time no longer seemed important. What mattered was being in Him and with Him. It was not a question of feeling loved, but of being loved, which is the thread of life, the core of my being. I was there to wait for Him, to prepare for His coming and then to be open to all He had in store for me.

> Alonius said, "If only a man desired it for a single day from morning till night, he would be able to come to the measure of God."
> (SDF, p. 35, #3)

I was aware that I did not know how to love and yet I longed to love God through all my limitations. Weaknesses and blind spots did not matter any more because the invitation was His. He would love in and through me. He would enable my tiny heart to burst outside its boundaries to love all He loves.

This led me to recognize Him in the trees and little animals, in the wildflowers and the woodland scents, in the sunlight and in the rain, in every germ of life. I could meet Him everywhere and I wanted to dance and sing to my Creator.

He was there, too, in the thoughtful kindness and knowing smiles of the hermits and those involved in the desert experience, in all the goodness I experienced around me.

He waited for me in the silence and also in the darkness, and I could touch Him in the pain of my struggles. I could hear Him say: "Remember, you can't do anything alone. Trust and let go in total surrender and you will live through the power of My resurrection."

He was there in the liturgies, in His Word listened to and pondered throughout the day, a listening with my heart rather than my head. "You can know Me only through loving" was a constant theme.

Daily Eucharist was a climax, a celebration with all the Church, with all my brothers and sisters throughout the world, a celebration of God's enormous love for each of us individually and personally. It was a surrendering of myself to Jesus in order to love Him and to make my life an intercession for all.

What I lived in the hermitage is, in a nutshell, the content and focus of my life wherever I am and in whatever circumstances.

Jesus is there in the wind and the rain falling on the roofs of our big city. This Life is there opening the red petals on my geranium plant in the back yard and in my neighbor's window box across the street.

I can recognize His face in the eager faces of the kids rushing to catch the school bus and in the smile of the conductor as he helps an elderly lady to her seat. He is there in all that is good, in every gesture of kindness, in every wise and thoughtful word, in every action which is open and welcoming to another. I can praise and celebrate Him in all the seemingly insignificant daily events which reveal His love and life.

I can see His word unfolded as I read the parables of life in the lives of my neighbors and friends: a new baby, a meal, an encounter, Johnny and Kathleen playing marbles on the stairway, the lady across the landing sharing a bargain from the supermarket. I can see Him in Anne's endurance to go on struggling with such a small allowance and not giving up her search to improve her situation. He is there in Jack's expression at the end of a boring and heavy day in the factory which read, "I'm more than this inhuman job." He is there in every seed of hope. That is resurrection.

I recognize Him, too, in a different but very special way in the eyes of the man at the corner of our street with his empty beer can and lost regard. In him I see the suffering Jesus.

Lord, open my eyes to see You everywhere, in all things, in each person, especially the poorest. Lord, open my heart through faith and love to recognize what is truly important, to love and to intercede so that all those You have created and loved may make their home in You for ever so that together we may praise You without end.

Little Sister of Jesus, England

Awareness of God's Presence

The sense that God really is present in all creation and in particular the woodlands, fields and structures that surround the physical hermitage of Bethlehem, has led me to know that He is also present within each one, in the spiritual Bethlehem.

> "Excuse me," said an ocean fish. "You are older than I, so can you tell me where to find this thing they call the ocean?" "The ocean," said the older fish, "is the thing you are in now." "Oh, this? But this is water. What I'm seeking is the ocean," said the disappointed fish as he swam away to search elsewhere.
>
> (SB, p. 12)

While I cannot spend more than limited times in the physical Bethlehem, the spiritual Bethlehem remains in me at all times — a constant, dependable source of peace and the knowledge that God is truly present.

> An elderly hermit once asked in his prayer for God to show him all of the ancient Fathers of the desert. He was then shown all of them except for St. Anthony the Great. "Wait! Where is St. Anthony?" he questioned with astonishment. "Where God is," he heard a voice assuring him.
>
> (LOVE, p. 55)

It is important to maintain a sense of the presence of God in our daily lives, not just during the times we are on retreat. One helpful practice is to maintain set times of the day for prayer; for instance: upon rising, driving to the office, at lunch time, while driving home and finally upon retiring. A similar schedule can be worked out by anyone. The key is to develop the habit based upon certain repetitious daily events.

Husband, Father, Lawyer

Messages from the Lord

I've always been very blessed during my times at the hermitage, but two experiences stand out most clearly.

During my first experience, I met the Desert Father. We discovered a lot in common. Father had a deep understanding of the need for ministry to families. He affirmed our mission and promised to pray for me on a committed basis. He also shared with the other retreatants about Families In Christ and asked them to join him in prayer for us. That commitment to prayer and Father's friendship has been an ongoing source of grace.

Included among the retreatants was a young woman. I met her again some years later through a mutual friend who suggested that she would be a wonderful addition to our team preparing families to adopt Mexican orphans. At the time of my first meeting with her, I shared the type of mission on which we sensed God was calling us. After a few days to consider our invitation, she agreed to join our team. Then she smiled at me and said, "You don't remember me, but I was at the hermitage when you began Families In Christ. I always had a strong urge to serve families and was at the hermitage to discern how I should respond. I made a commitment to pray for your ministry and have continued to pray since that time." I looked at her, a little speechless. Here we were seven years later, with the circle of God's direction now complete. The wonderful ways of our loving God never fail to amaze me.

The second experience took place a few months later. I entered my hermitage, remembering past blessings, but very tired physically and carrying a heavy agenda of *things to do* on my mind. One day of silence and rest began to give me some perspective, leaving room for God's works.

I was drawn strongly by the Spirit to spend hours in Eucharistic Adoration. With enough time to bathe in the Real Presence of Jesus, I sensed two clear prophetic messages:

— "You are My beloved friend."

— "It is time spent in the presence of pure Love which heals the broken heart and clears the confused mind."

These came not as neon signs, but as a gentle voice in my heart after hours of being with Jesus. Although it will take years to digest the full meaning of God's messages, let me share what I can understand now.

Three monks met unexpectedly at the river bank and one of them said, "I ask as a gift from God that we should arrive at our destination without fatigue in the power of the Spirit." Scarcely had he prayed when a boat was found ready to sail together with a favorable wind and in the twinkling of an eye they found themselves at their destination, although they were travelling upstream. (DRDF, p. 89)

"Beloved friendship" is the intimacy which Jesus came to create between us and God. All loving friendship has a healing quality, but when your friend is God Himself, the healing can go to the roots of your pain and sin. My beloved Friend, Jesus, is calling me to spend quality time in His presence, allowing Him to soak me in His healing light. That healing goes deeper than our own capacity to minister and touches the roots of my inner brokenness and poverty.

These messages are not just for me or a chosen few. They are for all of us seeking more freedom and a deeper capacity to love. Jesus is calling us to spend time, quality time, in His healing presence to touch the roots of what drives us away from God. He wants us free, on the inside of our being.

"When the Son frees you, you will really be free" (Jn 8:36).

The presence of God is found when we experience love and

those situations which are authored by God. This might be a special friendship, sacramental celebrations, the Scriptures, community praise and worship, Christian service, fine music, personal prayer or even a special place in nature. While all of these are ways to touch God, my recent experience before the Eucharist brought me to the awesome reality that I was face to face with Jesus. His presence is pure love.

"So I will lure you; I will lead you into the desert and speak to your heart. . . I will espouse you to Me forever: I will espouse you in right and in justice, in love and in mercy; I will espouse you in fidelity, and you shall know the Lord" (Ho 2:16, 22).

In the Old Testament, the *desert* described by Hosea is much more than a place of physical dryness — it is also a place where we encounter the awesome presence of the Holy One. I pray that you may find your desert place and soak in God's healing Love — the pure Love of Jesus, our beloved Friend.

Husband, Father, Director of Families In Christ

The Bread of Creation

"God looked at everything that He made and found it very pleasing" (Gn 1:31). God made me in His image and likeness and so I, too, can look at everything and, with the eyes of the God dwelling within me, see and say — all that God created is very pleasing indeed.

"In Him we live and move and have our being" (Ac 17:28). This can be said of everything God created on earth from the tiniest insect to the greatest mountain, the sky and the ocean, all the birds and fishes and every animal and plant. How much they all give glory to God by being exactly what God created them for and intended them to be. Man draws closer to his Creator by listening, seeing and pondering all these things in his heart and in an ecstasy of love crying out with the psalmist, "Lord God, how great You are!" For me it is the greatest lesson in humility to think that God, Who can make a sun and moon and all the celestial bodies, can take delight Himself and give delight to me in watching a little caterpillar cross from one side of the road to the other with fierce confidence that he will reach his goal because a force beyond himself is giving him the power and energy to move and be a caterpillar. "All the works of His hands speak of Him" (Ps 19:1).

The rain, the crickets, the birds, the animals, the wind and all that God created speak to me with the voices and the sounds that God has gifted them with. They are always in harmony, but unique. They understand and recognize each other. But do I — made in God's image and likeness — always speak in harmony and recognize the voice and see the image of Him in my brother and sister? Do I speak His language at all times in harmony with them? Or do I, who am free to choose, make myself the creator and God the creature because I see myself as greater than the caterpillar?

"Let all creation bless the Lord, praise Him and magnify Him forever" (Dn 3:57).

Hermit of Bethlehem

His Presence in Creation and Creativity

I come to Bethlehem like a traveller from a foreign land, my luggage bursting with immense love for my husband, my two children, and countless friends, packed tightly together with my own personal fears, financial burdens, and creative frustration in a world that doesn't understand. It takes my whole strength to pull myself away from my responsibilities as wife, mother, businesswoman and artistic director, to make the trip to the hermitage. Some hope in me dares to believe He is calling me, out of the marketplace into the desert, to find rest in His regenerative Love. And so, I go.

A certain philosopher questioned the holy Antony, "How can you be content, Father, without the comfort of books?" He replied, "My book, O philosopher, is the nature of created things and whenever I wish to read the words of God, it is in my hands." (DRDF, p. 77)

As soon as I step onto the forest floor of pine, and smell the sweetness of the damp woods on my way to my hermitage, the Silence envelops me, urging me to lay my luggage down and be still and see that after all, He is God. I take a long walk down the road, through the woods, into the bird sanctuary — and I take all my loved ones with me. One by one, I confide them to the Lord of the sky, Lord of the gentle birch and giant pine, goldfinch, geese and deer. I talk myself out, telling Him for the hundredth time, all their hopes, troubles and needs, as well as my own, until I have nothing more to say. Then I really begin to see and hear the lush perfection of God's creation all around me. I begin to enter the Silence.

In the chapel, the Silence is total. There, I am privileged to enter the deep prayer of the hermits. From the liturgy of the Mass at dawn to the descent of darkness, their total presence to God leads me to quiet. Gradually, I come to a still point — the Divine Spring of Creativity — where I lose all sense of my own struggle in the abundance of His Love. I begin to consider not my exhausting efforts to be this or to accomplish that, or even to empower others in great need, but the vastness and intimacy of the Divine Milieu where God is at work, creating and recreating through all my efforts and all my failures.

The whole of creation, and my place in it, is renewed in my understanding. I become a child again, dancing before the Lord, singing to Him with joy in my heart. I go back, as it were, to the original desire that made me want to create, and in spite of all the deep disappointments in my life, that desire sends forth new green shoots. I realize that He Who creates and sustains the entire universe has no need of me to create anything, but He chooses to use me as an instrument of His own Creative Love. The circumstances may change from year to year, yet His longing to be creative — to love His world in a very specific way through me — is a constant source of wonder. I am flooded with a sense of my own unworthiness, but at the same time, overwhelmed with gratitude that He should trust me with so much.

In the silence of my hermitage, He speaks. Through a sudden insight while reading the Bible; at a simple meal taken alone in His

Presence; in a dream; He makes Himself known. His Presence is calming, reassuring, affirming. He does not kick the stones or count the weeds in the garden of my heart. He lets me know He finds equal pleasure in the climbing roses and cascading clematis, the hard-to-grow delphinium and carefree daisies I have tried to nourish there. Tears of gratitude flow, and I feel free for the first time in months. Creating and nourishing is *not* all up to me. I have only to remain very still and watch the Divine Gardener make things grow.

> An old man said: "If you have words, but no work, you are like a tree with leaves but no fruit. But just as a tree bearing fruit is also leafy, a person who has good work comes up with good words."
>
> (DW, p. 40)

The day comes when I must leave Bethlehem. I am rested now, my luggage light and my purpose clear. I have been pruned, perhaps, but I am stronger for it. I know more surely than ever before how much He loves me, how totally He is with me. I have been given courage to face the daily struggles and make of them new seeds of new plants that may one day give Him pleasure. Most of all, I drive away absolutely sure that He will be there, waiting for me in all things, creating a lush and lovely garden out of a world that doesn't understand.

> When Abba Arsenius was still at the palace, he prayed the Lord saying: "Lord, show me the way to salvation." And a voice came to him: "Arsenius, run from men and you shall be saved." He went to become a monk, and again prayed in the same words. And he heard a voice saying: "Arsenius, be solitary; be silent; be at rest. These are the roots of a life without sin."
>
> (WA, p. 40, #3)

I try to return daily to the Silence and Creative Source that is Bethlehem. I have a favorite spot by a window, facing a dogwood tree,

15

where birds play in the branches all year 'round. There, I sit on the floor, immerse myself in the miracle of the new day, close my eyes and try to center my heart. This time of meditation brings me back to the Source of all Creative Life, a kind of mini-retreat before I go forward to begin a hectic schedule.

Many times during the day, when pressure mounts, conflicts arise, and I lose all perspective, I stop what I am doing and *quick-center* on the Creator of my life at work right now. Instantly, I am back at Behtlehem. I am hit with the realization of the uniqueness of this moment and I say a simple "Here I am, Lord. It's me. Is that you?"

What is absolutely amazing to me is that over a period of years, I have *returned to Bethlehem* like this, thousands and thousands of times, and always, these moments are powerhouses of calm, courage and love. The total creative renewal that is Bethlehem is not just a one-time thing; it is a vibrant reality that carries me through all the births and deaths and rebirths of daily life. Bethlehem has become for me, indeed, my daily bread.

And with all this in mind, what are some of the things Bethlehem means to me?

A place of absolute security in God's loving care where I can take refuge — and return again and again in my imagination — in the midst of sometimes overwhelming pressures and burdens in the world.

Abbot Anthony said: "Just as fish die if they remain on dry land, so monks remaining away from their cells, or dwelling with men of the world, lose their determination to persevere in solitary prayer. Therefore, just as the fish should go back to the sea, so we must return to our cells, lest remaining outside we forget to watch over ourselves interiorly." (WD, p. 29)

A time of letting go and becoming a child again — *being still* with the Lord as my best friend Who knows and cares for everything and everyone, with all the time in the world to hear me out — and to assure me of His Love.

A presence that is so palpable, so real, so all-enveloping, that no crisis is too big, no fear too debilitating, no rejection so total, no responsibilities too great, that He will not give me the strength and the vision to bear them.

An experience of unconditional love — so evident in the song of the birds, the smell of the pine needles, the unabashed beauty of the wildflowers, the peace of the woods, and most of all, the utterly selfless care of the hermits that brings me back to the One Thing Necessary: taking time to sit at His Feet and love Him.

Mother, Wife, Businesswoman, Artistic Director

Silence is Like God

What can you say about silence? It seems that as soon as you speak about silence, it is broken and its power is diminished. Yet it was the invitation to silence and solitude which drew me to Bethlehem in the first place. I knew God would speak, but I was somewhat anxious nevertheless at the beginning of the retreat. What I experienced was nothing less than the loving Heart of Jesus guiding me closer to Himself. Each day brought a new conviction that the Lord was with me. It was not always easy; I needed to confront myself in a truthful way. But always, always, the Lord was there, sometimes healing, sometimes challenging, sometimes reconciling.

Silence is like God. It simply *is*. I felt very real in silence. I have always loved quiet time for prayer, but I never felt the need for a greater discipline of silence in my life as Bethlehem taught me.

My very busy life can easily lead me astray from constantly confronting my false self with the living God. I know that silence and solitude will help me stay on the right track. In the quiet of the hermitage, faith, hope and love are nourished. While I cannot spend my whole life in silence and solitude because I have been called elsewhere, Bethlehem will always remain a special place.

> *Abba Joseph asked Abba Nisteros, "What should I do about my tongue, for I cannot control it?" The old man said to him, "When you speak, do you find peace?" He replied, "No." The old man said to him, "If you do not find peace, why do you speak? Be silent, and when a conversation takes place, prefer to listen rather than to talk."*
>
> (DRDF, p. 26)

Like any need, silence requires a discipline. One of the first things we need to do is catch ourselves as to how very quickly we fill up silent time. We wake up in the morning and turn on the television. We shave or bathe to music from the radio. Already our soul, our spiritual sense, is being scattered. We need to begin our day leisurely. This doesn't mean slowly; rather, it means in a recollected, reflective disposition. Turn *nothing* on when you rise in the morning. Let the first word you hear be the Word, Jesus Christ. As you get yourself together, think of Him. You will find it much easier, once you are dressed and prepared for the day, to spend some minutes doing nothing but being in His presence.

It is foolish to say that time is not a problem; we live in a very busy world, and there is much to do. But while making time is a challenge, it is not *the* problem. The problem is believing that *doing nothing but being* in the presence of the Lord is, in truth, the most important act of the day. For those who recite the Liturgy of the Hours daily, silent time after the Office is completed is most beneficial. This will allow the Word just prayed to go more deeply within. Remaining in church for a few minutes after Mass is a great way to "remain in Him as He remains in us." Just pausing after already scheduled opportunities for prayer, such as praying the Rosary or the Scriptures, helps to provide more time to give to the Lord, and yet it is at a time already offered to Him. The main point is the discipline of this; it must be a daily event. If we can do this at the same time each day, that is more beneficial. But we will need to be flexible, because our daily schedule fluctuates so much. That is why morning and evening are usually the best times for this. But if you value silence for the spiritual discipline it is, you will see to it daily. And God is more praised by your willingness to adjust your schedule for love of Him, than by demanding that it be done each day at the exact same time.

Diocesan Priest

Wondrous Encounter

Bethlehem — Womb of Silence, a place to be reborn. And there, in the enveloping silence, to be recreated; to be given a new name which no one else can read save the God Who gives it. How to describe the fullness of that solitude? — soul overflowing; sometimes desert; sometimes blossoming; searching, finding, yearning, replete, in that wordless unbroken quiet; His presence so strong yet not palpable as at other times; joy is that sparse cabin; alone yet never alone; happiness; oneness; peace; no desires; no wants; no expectations; just being in Him; knowing Him at a level other than sense but more surely and completely, with neither tiredness nor boredom nor tedium.

For the brief span of one week, I possessed a clarity of vision, an ability to see beyond the appearances. The inner life leapt into vigor, fed on the silence and solitude. Truly, His voice can only be heard in the quieting of the senses, inwardly and outwardly.

Thus Bethlehem set the stage for a wondrous encounter. In that honed-down-to-the-essentials cabin; through the daylight hours of complete solitude; into the soundless night, He could be found. Every space spoke eloquently of His Presence: the fields where the gentle deer fed; the forest with its endless path; the hermitage with its peacefulness; the chapel with our Eucharistic Lord. Such utter joy that solitude bestowed!

It may seem strange that one called to the *active* apostolate should relish this time alone. Yet my soul drank it in like the parched earth absorbs the gentle rain. The peace of Bethlehem settled in my spirit, filled it to its very depths, and took possession of my being. There was no room for fear in this aloneness, devoid of props and hiding places. Hurry and pressure were alien terms. Phones did not ring; demands were not made. There were no deadlines hanging over me or TV or radio to distract me. Even ordinary conversation was absent. Inner and outer noise ceased. Inside of myself I was as bare and empty as that hermitage.

Into my cleared-of-clutter abode, the Lord entered in and took up residence, till He filled the emptiness with Himself. It was a real *hands on* experience of the sufficiency of Our Lord to satisfy all our longings and meet all our needs. As a religious consecrated to Him, hadn't I learned all this long ago? Perhaps intellectually, but this was more a matter of the heart where that lesson was imparted convincingly.

> *Abba Poemen also said, "If you are silent, you will have peace wherever you live."* (SDF, p. 178, #84)

Though I have a daily schedule of prayer and work and rest, my life too can sometimes get caught up in the *so much to do* syndrome, with expectations — with compromises that nibble away that inner life so essential to spiritual survival. Immersed in the busyness of the daily grind, one can lose sight of the very meaning of this life. Thus Bethlehem becomes the pause that refreshes; a recall of the why of our existence and His purpose for our lives. It is a time to stop and take inventory; to readjust our perspective; to re-chart our inner compass lest we lose our way.

We need solitude and silence. The hermitage must perforce be carried along through work and travel and communication, much like the little hermit crab which carries its house wherever it goes and withdraws into it frequently to let the shell protect it from outward harm.

The hermitage is not so much a physical space as a state of mind; an habitual attitude of reflection and contemplation that becomes a source of enrichment for all and endows the spirit with a serenity that radiates peace. Using the off-mode for radio, TV, and CD player allows us to tune into the Lord's voice on a daily basis so that our relationship with Him can be continually nurtured. Often we find ourselves waiting — in traffic, for an appointment, on line anywhere, on hold. Instead of becoming impatient, the time could well be spent as a mini retreat by gathering our inner self and focusing attention on Our Lord in the center of our being. It takes a moment and can carry us along till we are gifted with those longer periods of uninterrupted reflection.

Let us carry the rich silence of Bethlehem Hermitage within, so that the Christ can be enfleshed in us and we may bring Him to all those to whom we minister each day.

Salesian Sister of St. John Bosco

God's Nurturing Love

Surprise registered on many faces when I shared with them the type of retreat I was about to live. "Unimaginable" was the thought of living a whole week in solitary silence with a day of *desert* in between. Thence followed the quizzical looks and uncomprehending smiles.

But since I am a somewhat independent soul, off I went to Bethlehem Hermitage. My only expectation was to spend a week alone with Our Lord. Since I had no other expectations but this, nothing surprised me or disappointed me as I let the ebb and flow of each day fill my spirit with its own gifts.

As a point of departure, I want to assure you that Jesus is a very good Companion. He never left me alone; He was always there to help me; He was consistently available; and what He had to say was ever meaningful and appropriate to the need of the moment. At no point did I feel lonely in that unbroken solitude that was so pregnant with His Presence.

SOLITUDE: This is the message of Bethlehem Hermitage. A message sorely needed by our society today and by we Salesian Sisters too. It is in this sacred solitude that His voice can be heard and communication takes place at a deeper level, thus strengthening and fortifying our relationship with Him. What a freeing experience solitude affords, as the walls of space and time disappear, enlarging the soul's capacity to listen, learn and love. Is it really so strange to take one week out of the 52 and spend it totally with the One Who is our very Life?

> Amma Syncletica said, "It is possible to be a solitary in one's mind while living in a crowd, and it is possible for one who is a solitary to live in the crowd of his own thoughts." (SDF, p. 234, #19)

This time at Bethlehem enabled me to appreciate even more the joy our cofoundress Mary Mazzarello felt as she worked in the silent fields of Mornese or watched at her solitary window, or walked to Mass in the pre-dawn silence of the countryside.

What a gift to us are these hermits and this hermitage that offer cordial, hidden hospitality to their more outwardly active brothers and sisters on the journey. They afford us the possibility to stop the frenetic pace of our lives in a radical way so that we can readjust our vision and our attitude. It does take a great deal of determined courage to live alone, even if only for a week, and to come face to face with ourselves in His Presence with nowhere to hide; with no props and certainly, with no excuses. It is a searing yet healing experience.

Were the days long? I tell you honestly, there did not seem time enough on any day and they passed all too rapidly. Reading consisted solely of the Bible. Boring? It was as though I were reading it for the first time, so refreshing and full of meaning were its pages. My assigned hermitage became my Bethlehem cradle, as its very walls and simplicity created a tangible symbol of God's nurturing love.

How I relished being in that little cabin, looking out upon a world at peace and oneness with its Creator! It's very hard to put into words all that transpired in the secret of my heart during my week there. I want to publicly thank God and my Provincial Superior for giving me

22

this precious opportunity and one of my Salesian Sisters for sharing with me her Hermitage experience which whet my thirst to go there too. How can I thank the hermits who courageously and joyously live this hidden life each day? Words cannot express my gratitude for all they have been to me. I offer my prayer that they may continue on the Way, accompanied by many others who hear the call of Bethlehem.

Salesian Sister of St. John Bosco

Just "Being"

It was in 1981 that I visited Bethlehem Hermitage for the first time, and I returned 10 years later to find a Laura of hermits rather than a staff.

There is a sense of purpose, of belonging, and steadiness, and it became clear to me that the Laura was deeply rooted in God. A tree is planted, the roots are pushing deeper and deeper in the earth, and birds can nestle in the branches. So, for one week I settled there among the trees, to take advantage of that outer space, to enter deeper into the inner space. The deep silence surrounded me, enveloped me, wrapped me up, so the God of silence could reach me. God needs our silent heart to be heard, and a silent nature is all the more conducive to the profound, real encounter.

The eremitic pace of life there invited me to switch my own pace. No need to rush, to run, to do, just become silent, slow, but alert, open and listen!

I listened to the silence, to God, and to my heart. And I spent many, many quiet hours, not reading, just *being*; listening, admiring the beauty around me, my body at rest too in such a pleasant setting.

Back at home I have discovered my back porch can be my little Bethlehem, where I can admire the birds, flowers and foliage. My own *Holy Ground* because God is present here. The experience of Bethlehem was so profound that I need to cultivate it by times of silent adoration, Scripture reading and meditation in my Bethlehem where I live today — one day at a time. "Everything is grace," says St. Paul, and my stay at the hermitage was just such a grace. I have not been the same since I was there.

Little Sister of Jesus

A Waiting Silence

The most obvious quality that people notice and feel about a hermitage is its silence. This is not merely the silence of the place, or even the silence of the hermit in his cell; very often it's the silence of God. We go to a hermitage expecting to hear God's voice, and when all we get is silence we're surprised and shocked. It's easy to doubt one's faith at such moments. We're disappointed with God. We expected better of Him. After all, we've gone to considerable time and trouble to establish contact with the Holy One. We begin to wonder if there's something wrong with us that makes God unwilling to show Himself. Or (worse yet) maybe this whole God-thing is a delusion. Even people with a lifelong commitment to their faith can begin to doubt it when they come up against a silence that is so complete, so deep, and in response to such earnest pleading.

I remember the story the Desert Father told about himself when, as a seminarian, he went through a time of arid meditation. In response, his spiritual director told him simply to lengthen the time of meditation. The answer to silence, it seems, is more of the same. It's hard for those of us who visit for short spells to *break through* God's silence by extending our periods of prayer. But even in a few days we encounter God's silence in a manner that will stay with us long after we leave. Bethlehem Hermitage is different. When we're away from it, in the confusion of our daily occupations, we *don't hear* God because we're not listening or haven't got time to listen. His silence is a sign of absence or irrelevance. When we're at the hermitage we *don't hear* God because we are listening. His silence then is a sign of His mystery. His silence becomes revelation.

> *A brother in Scetis went to ask for a word from Abba Moses and the old man said to him, "Go and sit in your cell and your cell will teach you everything."*
>
> (DRDF, p. 38)

After we get past the first shock of it, the silence of God has its own particular character. It's a *waiting silence* — the kind of silence, for instance, one experiences in a room during the moment before someone speaks. Lying in my hermitage at night I hear the hunters' guns in the woods, and I reflect that God's silence is not the silence that sweeps in after the explosion, but the silence that builds up before the next one. It's a different quality of silence.

The second great lesson we learn is how to break the silence. If this silence has a deep and sacred quality, then the first word spoken to break the silence is crucially important. It falls on us like thunder. At Bethlehem the silence is often broken by a phrase from the liturgy or Scripture. We who have been waiting with some disappointment for God to break His silence are often jerked awake when the first words of worship sweep over us. The shepherds at the first Bethlehem must have felt something of that shock when their silence was interrupted by angels.

God's silence will always remain a problem. It's disappointing, annoying, uncalled-for, yet also mysterious and appealing. His silence is more profound than ours. Often we leave Bethlehem with still no word from Him. But at least the silence is more tangible. To use a common expression, *it grows on us*, and we know God is inside it somewhere. We leave Bethlehem with the feeling that we have become the silence. We have become, ourselves, hermitages where God sits in silence, and His silence has become our Word.

One can learn the discipline of silence by faithfully reflecting on God's presence in word and works, and take the time to listen and wait patiently for His answer. One would grow in awareness of this lived reality and may even try to extend these valuable periods of silence alone with the Alone.

Layman, Husband, Father, Editor

The Desert Within

Bethlehem is a place of expectant waiting; where one waits for God to speak and for the quieting of an anxious heart that, only then, can listen.

Bethlehem was a place where, upon arrival, I had to endure the frustration of many interior distractions — the fruit of being continually bombarded with the sounds and images that pervade everyday life in our society. But soon after, it became a place where I could experience an inner sense of silence and peace.

I discovered firsthand that Bethlehem was not a beach experience but a desert experience; not a place of vacation but of purification. Bethlehem provided many opportunities for rest and relaxation but it was a vigilant and expectant relaxation; a rest that is alert and open to recognize the promptings of the Spirit; a rest that is honest in self-examination and determined on allowing God to be the Master of the retreat experience.

For me, the hermitage was a place I approached with some fear and trembling but ultimately with faith and trust. I knew it was a place that gave God plenty of room to do His work of transformation. This sometimes hurts — thus the fear and trembling.

Bethlehem is a place where an arrogant and fragile self-assurance is replaced with a more firm and lasting assurance in God. It is a place of death for the self-boasting ego and rebirth for the part of us that not only recognizes our true and dependent state before God but rejoices in it!

At Bethlehem, I discovered more profoundly the presence of Jesus living within me — like the Child Jesus in the stable. It was a place that challenged me not to let this Child's cries for attention go unheard; not to let this Child die of neglect or malnourishment.

My experience of Bethlehem was a genuine experience of solitude. Hidden in a remote area in Chester, New Jersey, I found surprisingly fertile ground for a profound encounter with my truest self and the One True God.

One may create a hermitage experience in any everyday life. Silence of the heart and tongue will help. The call of solitude may be answered by finding a place at home or at work where one can seek the desert within.

Diocesan Priest

The Paschal Mystery

The invitation into the Paschal Mystery is a journey process of dying in order to be reborn. It comes to one many times in life, and on many levels. In varied circumstances — some serious and some not so serious, in horrendous soul-wrenching trials or small, minor events — the dying to self, the destruction of the false ego, takes place. St. John of the Cross says, "I die daily, but I do not die."

The Paschal Mystery is an invitation from the Uncreated One to all men and women. It is global, it is timeless. It has been so since the beginning of time, and will be so until the end of time.

Yet, this dying to self is a unique experience for each person. God, in His loving mercy, tailors the events in our lives in a way that will speak to the root of sinfulness that is unique to each individual. God made each one of us because He wanted us, and this relationship with Him is expertly designed to empty and heal each soul according to their individual personalities. Grace does not intrude upon nature; the workings of this mystery leave the personality intact, but purified to such a degree that a relationship of love with the Uncreated One is then possible.

Abba John gave this advice: "Watching means to sit in the cell and be always mindful of God. This is what is meant by, 'I was on the watch and God came to me.'" (SDF, p. 91, #27)

Jesus Christ came as the model for this process. He is the innocent Lamb of God led to the slaughter. We are not innocent, yet our daily dying is offered back to the Father in love, in trust and in surrender.

I have experienced this personally through the death of my daughter. She was 18 years old and a freshman in college when she was killed. Dealing with the horror and shock, the loss and the grief, were all part of a physical and psychological process that has taken years of work and is still going on. Spiritually the process is one of letting go, of surrender, of trust. It is a dying to self, and saying, "Yes, I will let God be the kind of God that He wants to be to me. I will not confine Him to my petty and controlling idea of who He should be. I will let Him be sovereign in my life."

Christ came to demonstrate this very Truth. Only by dying to myself can I enter into and participate in the Paschal Mystery. The silence and solitude of the hermitage enhances the opportunity for the dialogue between the creature and the Creator to take place. I had come to a point of being angry with God; I was bitter and resentful. My spiritual director told me to take a crucifix in my hands during prayer time and look at it, and tell Jesus exactly how angry I was and how unfairly I thought I had been treated. As I looked at the body of Jesus, helplessly nailed to the wooden cross, I began to rail and complain about all of my frustrations — out loud.

> Abba Poemen said: "Whatever travail comes upon you shall be overcome by silence." (WA, p. 177, #9)

As I heard my own rancorous words, my eyes focused on this broken, bleeding body of the God-Man crucified. I began somehow to understand that Christ was inviting me to join Him in His suffering and death that is the Paschal Mystery. He was looking to me for solace, for *my* support in His suffering and crucifixion. He and I were one in this experience of suffering and dying. Even though in time our experiences were separated by almost 2000 years, we were suffering and dying simultaneously. It seemed to me that we were united in a mystery that was willed by the Father. "Father, somehow let this cup pass from me if possible; if not, let Thy will not mine be done" (Mt 26:42).

For me it was a moment of knowledge that my will and Jesus' will were one in union with the will of the Father. I believe that the invitation to enter into the Paschal Mystery is an invitation to enter into the mystery of Triune Life, the Life of the Holy Trinity itself. Our simultaneous crucifixions were merging into one sacrifice offered to the Father in supplication for the salvation of all. I, now, no longer suffered alone; Jesus was there with me. Further, He and I were united to all who suffer and die, and this, I believe, is the Paschal Mystery. This union transcends time and space, and is eternally viable. All suffering, whether it is major or minor, whether it is small scratches or excavations at the depths of one's inner core, all are part of the power and the energy that is the Paschal Mystery. It is, however, a grace that we must be open to receive; it is a gift that the Father desires to give each one of us. This truly is the Mystery of Life, and it leads us to Life Everlasting.

Wife, Mother and Spiritual Directress

Deserts

Deserts come in many different physical forms and environments. The desert is the place to which we are led in response to the call of the Spirit. It is the place in which we are tempted by Satan. It is the place where we are ministered to by the various kinds of angels the Spirit sends (Mk 1:13). For the hermit the physical setting is the hermitage; for the lay person the physical setting may be the home, the office, the halls of a courthouse or a bank, the floor of a factory. Spiritually it is the place in our heart and soul where we are experiencing our need for God, the place where we are formed or fashioned by temptation and the ministration of grace. It is the place where we experience the Paschal Mystery. It is the place where we identify with the incarnation, the life, the passion, the death, the resurrection and the glorification of Jesus Christ. It is the place where we make that Paschal Mystery our own.

He also said, "Poverty, hardship, austerity and fasting, such are the instruments of the solitary life. It is written, 'When these three men are together — Noah, Job and Daniel — there am I, says the Lord' (Ezk 14:14). Noah represents poverty; Job, suffering; and Daniel, discernment. So, if these three works are found in a man, the Lord dwells in him."

(SDF, p. 175, #60)

God has not called me to be a hermit or to be a religious. For me as a layman the desert is my home, my law office, the courtroom where I try a case, the public meeting room where I present my client's application. It is easy to lose sight of the fact that these are my *desert*. Faced with the pressures of family life, the stress of a law practice and the demands of clients, it is easy to become disoriented, to lose my way. The stress and problems of my everyday life can overwhelm me if I lose touch with the truth — this is my place of testing. This is my opportunity to change ordinary aggravation and problems into salvific suffering by identifying it with and uniting it to the paschal suffering of Jesus Christ.

But how easily I forget — how easily I get lost and disoriented — lost in the *wilderness*. I constantly need to remind myself and to pray for the grace to keep my focus on Jesus. When I become disoriented I need to remember what Jesus said and did for His disciples after their return from their first mission. He said, "You must come away to some lonely place all by yourselves and rest for a while" (Mk 6:31).

> Amma Syncletica said, "In the beginning there are a great many battles and a good deal of suffering for those who are advancing towards God and afterwards, ineffable joy. It is like those who wish to light a fire; at first they are choked by the smoke and cry, and by this means obtain what they seek (as it is said: 'Our God is a consuming fire' [Heb 12:24]); so we also must kindle the divine fire in ourselves through tears and hard work." (SDF, p. 230, #1)

In my life that *lonely place* is often Bethlehem. Jesus gives me the silent times to minister to me, to reorient myself to Him and restore my focus on the Paschal Mystery in my ordinary life. In the prayer and solitude of Bethlehem my God teaches me and prepares me to hear Him every day. He refreshes me to be able to live out the mission He has given to me not to be a hermit, but a husband, a father, a layman, a lawyer. He wants me to know that my desert is not just a place of testing, but a place where He ministers to me and loves me.

Husband, Father, Lawyer

Purity of Heart

The Christian existentialist, Sören Kierkegaard, wrote that purity of heart is to will one thing. And that one thing is the good — our Father's will — as no person created in God's image can totally will evil in this life.

So many of us are divided inside. We want to love God, but also money; we want to be humble, but also famous; we want to love those we live with, but are fed up with their faults endlessly hassling us. This divided life, this willing of two conflicting things at once, is the typical life of modern men and women.

Perhaps that is why people are stunned by their occasional encounters with the pure of heart. People who are used to being *a house divided against itself*, find the unity of purpose within the pure of heart attractive. To will one thing — the good, our Father's will — makes life so much simpler. We can slip off our heavy burdens filled with anxieties, conflicts, and semiconscious pulls that interfere with being one with God.

To be pure of heart, to have only one desire — the good, our Father's will — is a constant challenge. Our daily battleground is our families, jobs, and communities. We can become oblivious, clouded, confused. Life can become so busy that we need to regain perspective.

In the 1970's when I worked in a Catholic charismatic community, I frequently went to the desert-like solitude of the Bethlehem Hermitage to seek and to be found. God would do something. It was too deep to understand well, but it bore fruit. There would be fewer conflicts inside and the voices for anything other than the good, our Father's will, would be drained of their power. I found myself with more energy and happiness, as if less was being drained by short-circuiting.

> *Abba Ammoun of Rhaithou asked Abba Sisoes, "When I read the Scriptures, my mind is wholly concentrated on the words so that I may have something to say if I am asked." The old man said to him, "That is not necessary; it is better to enrich yourself through purity of spirit and to be without anxiety and then to speak."*
>
> (SDF, p. 216, #17)

I moved out of state for medical school, residency, medical work with Native Americans, and later, marriage and private practice. The lessons I learned from spending a long time in solitude, at Bethlehem Hermitage and elsewhere, remain with me now. I learned that every person I meet is the image of God, and I shouldn't let all the surface problems obscure it. I learned that every task I do can be done with love that draws me to God, or with resentment that blocks the way to God. I learned that the choices I make, make me.

The desert life forced me to confront my own divided life. For some, the desert life may be a lifetime calling, for others a period of their lives or a retreat. The spiritual battle going on in the world and within us can sometimes be seen more clearly in the desert. But we need to develop an apocalyptic vision that lets us see it everywhere as it really is.

I tell myself: Don't waste the desert experience. If God places you for a time in the desert — a retreat at Bethlehem, a term in prison, a confinement to a hospital or nursing-home bed — don't waste it. Seek and be found. Knock and be opened. Face the divisions inside that block purity of heart. Posture to be open to God's illumination and work.

> Amma Sarah said: "If I pray to God that all people might be inspired because of me, I would find myself repenting at the door of every house. I would rather pray that my heart be pure toward everybody." (DW, p. 91)

Don't wait for the desert. God wants to do something *now* in the midst of your life — in your relationships, jobs, choices:

— The people in your life are created in God's image. Locate God in them and reach out for Him. Love the people God has placed in your life. Don't be so disturbed about everyone's imperfections, including your own, that you miss the whole point of what God is doing.
— The jobs you have, be they major careers or minor tasks, can be done with love and care or with resentment and sloppiness. The attitudes you develop will either open you to God working *now* (the pure of heart will see God), or block you from seeing Him.
— The choices you make, make you. The dozens of little decisions you make every day, as well as the occasional

major life decisions, will shape the kind of person you are becoming. Pay attention to how God's Spirit is unfolding His plan for your life by the decisions He brings to you to make every day.

Husband, Father, Medical Doctor

Seeing All Things in God

"The ultimate goal of the eremitical life is the possession of God. . . the immediate goal of the hermit's desert journey is purity of heart."

Rule of the Hermits of Bethlehem

Many years ago, a retreat master told us that purity of conscience is the sincere desire not to offend God, but should we offend Him a hundred times a day, and offend Him seriously for years and years, we should not give up trying; ultimately we will reach the goal, provided we humbly and quickly repent of each fall, that we have confidence in God who suffered His Passion and Death for love of us.

Living as a hermit in a permanent atmosphere of solitude helps me better to see reality and all things in God, creating an inner spiritual transparency which I did not previously have, in which I am acutely aware of my past and present sins and infidelities which I had either hardly noticed or seriously considered. I now see them with greater clarity — more as God sees them. I do not allow them to overwhelm me, as I know I am loved by an infinitely merciful Father, Who is all kindness and tenderness to those who are truly repentant. In my daily falls I accept my weaknesses and poverty, loving my littleness; then peacefully go on trying, exercising confidence in the mercy of God each time.

St. Claude de la Colombiere said at the hour of death that he would rather have many serious sins than no sins so that God could exercise His mercy. According to St. Francis de Sales, if we fall 100 times a day and repent 100 times a day, we have purity of conscience more than another who may fall once a day but have no repentance. So I can never judge another because of his or her apparent falls, as they may be immediately repented of. Our faults and falls are motives for humility and an abiding compunction.

". . .we likewise bring every thought into captivity to make it obedient to Christ" (2 Cor 10:5).

"Keep your heart with all vigilance; for from it flows the springs of life" (Pr 4:23).

We can strive to achieve that delicacy of conscience which is not a scruple by keeping watch over our heart. A traditional attitude of desert spirituality is control of the thoughts by the frequent invocation of the Name of the Lord Jesus. We must love to reflect on Jesus' Passion, leading to His Resurrection and Union.

Some men visited a Desert Father and saw him praying in the wilderness. They asked, "What do you do out here, old man?" To which the Abba replied, "I am a shepherd." Looking around in the distance the men said, "But there are no sheep." "I shepherd my thoughts," was the reply. We shepherd our thoughts, keeping watch over what the Lord has entrusted to us, and leading all to Him. This is most true in the case of the heart, for all shepherding of thoughts is directed toward purity of heart, so that we might see God (cf. Mt 5:8).

Hermit of Bethlehem

Prayer: Entering the Mystery of His Love

Seeking a relationship with God, a striving to enter into the Mystery of His Love, is what prayer means to me. The prayer-filled silence of Bethlehem Hermitage is where this began in my spiritual journey.

"Be still and know that I am God" (Ps 46:10).

These words of the Psalmist spoke to me clearly during my retreat at the hermitage. Silence in prayer is as necessary to discover Who God is, as air is to the lungs. Yes, God can be imagined in a

35

torrential, sweeping force, an ineffable power that dominates, but most often He reveals Himself in the interior silence and innermost depths of my inner being, where He alone resides.

The exterior silence of my prayer leads to an interior silence of the mind and the will. Not speaking turns me in on myself so that I begin to discover who I am, and Who God is for me. This is the atmosphere where true prayer begins. The deep peacefulness that ensues enables my intellect and my heart to commune in the deepest levels of my being with the Uncreated One, Who is the very ground of my existence.

As this form of prayer becomes a lyrical dialogue between creature and Creator, I begin to surrender my ideas of who I think God is, and even my ideas of who I think I am, in order to discover Reality and Truth, to discover the Face of God, much like Moses and Elijah.

This type of prayer always involves a surrender, a complete willingness to let go of who and what I imagined my own reality to be, and to discover the person that God created me to be. This necessarily involves dealing with our own reality, letting go of our denial, and ultimately forgiving ourselves. This is truly a humbling experience, for it reveals to us our true sinfulness, and our creature-Creator relationship comes into even sharper focus. All of our former ideas, masks, and defenses have been shattered by the Loving Mercy of God. Sheldon Vanauken calls it "a severe Mercy."

> They said of Abba Arsenius that on Saturday evening he put his back to the setting sun and stretched out his hands towards heaven, and prayed until the dawn of the rising sun on Sunday lit up his face; and then he sat down again. (WA, p. 141, #1)

This prayer experience is much like the faint underwater sound of the submarine's *bleep-bleep*. It is distant and faint, but becomes stronger, louder, and a distinct reality as one moves near. This tiny signal is going off at the depths of my being, that deep, deep place where God alone resides, and as I move through this prayer experience He becomes more and more real, His voice becomes louder and louder.

> *Abba Nilus said, "Prayer is the seed of gentleness and the absence of anger."* (DRDF, p. 44)

I try to bring this experience of the hermitage home with me through the use of centering prayer at least 20 minutes a day. I incorporate it into my daily hour of prayer. Through centering, my mind and psyche are able to disgorge a lot of the accumulated load that they carry, and for 20 minutes I relieve the strain, so to speak, by imageless prayer. The distracting thoughts are just allowed to float by unheeded, as I focus on my prayer word, enabling me to rest in a quiet space in His Presence.

Wife, Mother, Spiritual Director

Bethlehem in My Home

As a result of my Bethlehem experience, my wife and I have named our own home "Bethlehem." We see Bethlehem as a place where Jesus is born and a place where He is welcome. As with any name or symbol, I believe that my family will grow in a depth of understanding of the meaning of the name Bethlehem — House of Bread and friendship, place of adoration and worship, poverty, homelessness, family, simplicity and quiet — and this will help us all to grow close to Him.

I pray that we and our children might grow in our desire and ability to welcome Jesus into our home. I also pray that the Lord Jesus will continue to bless the work at the hermitage with His Spirit of Bethlehem.

Husband, Father

Heart of the Matter

I want to let you know that, as a layman, I feel especially privileged to have been able to make a hermitage retreat. With facilities for so few, numerically the odds were against it. Then, too, a layperson known only by name and a few other particulars is not a likely volunteer to be plunged into a baptism of silence and prayer for a week.

Several earlier retreat experiences had prepared me for the formality of the hermitage experience — silence, liturgy, Eucharistic adoration, Scriptural meditation. But none had fully prepared me for the heart of the matter.

At Bethlehem, the matter is the heart, and the ultimate formality is the formless abandonment that must follow our acceptance of Paul's challenge to "pray without ceasing" (1 Th 5:17), while remembering his warning that "we do not know how to pray as we ought. . . but the Spirit prays for us" (Rm 8:26). At the hermitage I was able to experience for the first time what I had long known: to pray I must humbly wait in patient silence for the Spirit to speak to my heart.

There is a necessary tension here, a *war within me*. And it is a common aphorism that the purpose of ministry is to comfort the afflicted and afflict the comfortable. When I (reluctantly) left the hermitage, I was comfortably afflicted. I am still. And I am still in Bethlehem. And Bethlehem is still in me.

Layman, Engineer

Touching the Spirit

I have made two four-day retreats in solitude at Bethlehem Hermitage. I want to thank Jesus and the Blessed Mother and St. Joseph for leading me there and allowing me to share in the life and spirituality of the hermits.

I found my days in solitude both spiritually uplifting and enjoyable. It was a time away from the hustle and bustle of a rather busy prison ministry. I do try to make prayer, Mass, spiritual reading and some fasting a priority in my daily life; otherwise I would be lost or burnt out. Without my spiritual life I would dry up and not have anything to give to others. I think *The Soul of the Apostolate* by Dom Chautard says that we are called to be reservoirs, not channels — a channel lets the water pass right through it, not retaining any, whereas a reservoir must be filled first in order to allow the overflow to benefit that which has need of water.

I, too, as an ordained instrument in Jesus' hands must be filled first in order to be really an effective tool of His. The solitude at Bethlehem helps me get my priorities in order. It helped me to empty the garbage and sludge in myself in order to allow the Father to fill me with the Holy Spirit, and thus hopefully to act more like Jesus in my dealings with others.

Diocesan Priest

Unique Serenade of Beauty

The hermitage experience offers an extremely efficacious opportunity for one to enter into a deeper relationship with God in the awesome silence and solitude of His creation. Just as the shepherds were drawn from their flocks, in order to adore Christ Jesus in the manger, so also are we called. "Come to Me all you who labor and find life burdensome and I will give you rest, for My yoke is easy and My burden is light" (Mt 11:28-30).

Bethlehem provides the unique opportunity to hear Him gently calling us by name, inviting us to give ourselves entirely to Him, trusting that He will care for our every need. Jesus asks us to surrender everything to His care and then sing, as the angels, to His glory, in loving adoration.

> Some monks came to see Abba Poemen and said to him, "When we see brothers dozing during the services in church, should we rouse them so that they can be watchful?" He said to them, "For my part, when I see a brother dozing, I put his head on my knees and let him rest."
>
> (DRDF, p. 45)

So often in the daily business of our lives we confuse the order of work and prayer. We find it so difficult to be still and realize the presence of God within us. Rather than prayer being the center of our lives, we treat it as another daily chore. Within the incredible silence of Bethlehem, God speaks directly to the heart. The Child in the manger, the Bread of Life speaks to us saying: "I love you infinitely! I forgive you infinitely! I want to be with you for all eternity!" How can our response be anything less than a consuming desire to love Him in return with all our heart, soul, mind and strength? He takes the weakness and frailty of our human hearts and creates with them a beautiful serenade for His glory.

> Abba Nilus said, "Everything you do in revenge against a brother who has harmed you will come back to your mind at the time of prayer."
>
> (DC, p. 153, #1)

The initial reaction to the hermitage can be one of fear. Strange though it may sound, the silence upon entering is so very foreign from our usual life that it is difficult to let go. There is no radio or television, no conversation or communication. Thus, instead of the usual distraction, one becomes totally aware of oneself within the presence of God. We realize our sinfulness and frailty before God. Yet, at the same time, He gives us an experience of His tender love and mercy.

Nourished by the daily reception of His Body and Blood in the Eucharist, our desire for Him is satiated by His gift of total self-giving. Furthermore, His Word teaches us, by the grace of the Holy Spirit, how to respond to this experience in our lives when we leave the hermitage. Thus we are able to take this contemplative prayer into our active duties.

The peace found in contemplative prayer is a gift which one will draw upon in the activity of everyday life. Here are some suggestions on how to maintain a deep contemplative prayer life after one returns to the hustle and bustle of life:

— Try to begin each day with a prayer devoting the day to Our Lord. Also, train yourself to say short prayers or ejaculations during those times where you find yourself between one task and the next. This will deepen your realization of the presence of God with you throughout the day; e.g., "Sacred Heart of Jesus, we implore that we may ever love you more and more."

— Try to set aside a certain time each day for private meditation on the Scriptures, either the readings for the Mass or else private study.

— If at all possible, try to get to Mass each day, for it is through the Eucharist that we receive life eternal.

— Either in the morning or in the evening, when the distractions are least, set aside time to place yourself in the presence of God in an act of love and adoration. Before this prayer time perhaps you could say the Bethlehem prayer and draw upon the graces received during your Bethlehem retreat.

Seminarian

Praying the Psalms as the Desert Fathers Did

The Liturgy of the Hours has evolved as the prayer of the Church with Christ and to Christ from its earliest beginnings in the common prayer of the first Christians, down through the ages to an ordered round of hours prayed by priests, communities and individual Catholic faithful throughout the world. The psalms, prayers, intercessions and readings allow groups and individuals to join their prayers through the power of the Holy Spirit to those of Christ and His Church in a great unity of praise, worship, thanksgiving, repentance and petition to the Father of us all. What a privilege I have experienced in using Morning Prayer of the Liturgy of the Hours as part of my own personal daily prayer. I no longer pray alone, but rather experience the unity of the Body of Christ, and even the Trinity, through the Holy Spirit as we praise our God and Father. As I pray the ancient psalms and contemplate the scriptural passages, I experience the richness of worship with God's faithful in Old and New Testament times. God's Word is true and convincing and encouraging and inspiring of gratitude for me today, as it is for my brothers and sisters of the Church throughout the world — and has been for God's faithful through the ages. Our hearts thrill together to the promise of God, the faithfulness, the mercy, and the love of God.

The brothers asked Abba Agatho, "Father, which virtue in our way of life needs most effort to acquire?" And he said to them, "Forgive me, I think nothing needs so much effort as prayer to God. If a man is wanting to pray, the demons infest him in the attempt to interrupt the prayer, for they know that prayer is the only thing that hinders them. All the other efforts of a religious life, whether they are made vehemently or gently, have room for a measure of rest. But we need to pray till we breathe out our dying breath. That is the great struggle." (WA, p. 141 #2)

My recent desert experience at Bethlehem stirred an even deeper love for the Liturgy of the Hours as we prayed Morning Prayer in common and in contemplative fashion, prayerfully savoring the message in the words, and concluding with a solemn doxology to the Father, the Son, and the Holy Spirit. The solitude of Bethlehem encouraged me to pray the Liturgy of the Hours at other times of the day as well, something my life in the world doesn't easily permit. The role of the hermit to constantly pray and intercede for the whole Church and the world is a tremendous grace and support for us in our active lives of service in the world. Now I often reflect on the prayer I know is being offered by the hermits throughout the day. I can join myself to their prayer and the prayer of the whole Church in union with Christ and the Holy Spirit.

The hermitage experience has helped me to pray the Morning Liturgy of the Hours in a more contemplative manner, allowing the Holy Spirit to work in my own heart through the words of the prayers. I allow time to *be* before the Lord — in quiet and solitude — to enjoy His presence and hear His Word for me. I try to hear His Word, too, by previewing the readings for the Mass of the day, so that the Eucharist begins at my Morning Prayer and makes a clearer impact as I hear the Word repeated at Mass itself.

During Lent or Advent, my family has tried to celebrate the season together by sharing night prayers from the Hours. We experience increased unity in prayer with Christ and His Church at these times — a wonderful way to celebrate liturgical seasons together. We've alternately tried reading from the Office of Readings together after dinner. This bears much fruit as we experience and reflect on the wealth of the Fathers of the Church. These are just a few ways to use the Liturgy of the Hours in daily or seasonal prayer.

Wife, Mother

Praying in the Lord

The Liturgy of the Hours is a school of continual prayer and an integral part of my life. During my retreats at Bethlehem, I have come to appreciate the Liturgy of the Hours as the prayer of the Church. The slow tempo of recitation during Vespers with the hermits has taught me to slow my tempo when reciting the Office. When taking part in the Office with them, I sensed a bonding among the group even though we never entered into conversation. At times God used the words of the Psalmist to speak to me. At other times, I felt joined to the Lord as He spoke the words to the Father. The Liturgy of the Hours was a preparation for silent, waiting prayer, as provided for by the period of contemplative prayer included in Solemn Vespers.

And this was just a beginning — the beginning of a practice to be carried into my daily schedule so that I rise earlier to pray the Office, now in my room instead of the hermitage, but before the same icon of the Trinity. The tempo is slower, with proper inclinations. The bonding now is spread to all members of the Church, particularly the students and faculty I meet each day, my family, community members, and friends. But wider still, I believe and hope that the Lord will use my prayer, both the Liturgy of the Hours and the periods of contemplative prayer, for souls, those in this time and place whom He desires. So it is with Him and in Him that I pray, "From the rising of the sun to its setting may the name of the Lord be praised" (Ps 113:3).

Dominican Sister, Amityville, New York

The Priest as Servant of God's Word

The daily life of a priest is, to a large extent, based on the Sacred Scriptures. The Word of God is a vital part of our teaching and our counseling as well as being the basis of our liturgical preaching. Yet in each of these ways, we are tempted to treat the Bible as simply a tool that we use. We study it, we dissect it and we explain it so that we can come to see ourselves as masters of a literary form rather than as servants of God's Word. The same temptations exist for all who make Scripture study a part of their spiritual life. We begin seeking nourishment from the bread of the Word, but we can lose sight of the ultimate goal.

One of the benefits of Bethlehem is that we can once again place ourselves at the table of the Word as God's children receiving nourishment from His plenitude. The very silence of Bethlehem cleanses our ears from the distracting noise of the outer world. For the time we are there, we need not explain the Word of God or find any fresh insights. We need not be eloquent and we need not show ourselves to be experts. Instead, we allow God to nourish us as we take time to reflect and digest the bread of the Word.

> Someone asked Abba Anthony, "What must one do in order to please God?" The old man replied, "Pay attention to what I tell you: whoever you may be, always have God before your eyes; whatever you do, do it according to the testimony of the Holy Scriptures; in whatever place you live, do not easily leave it. Keep these three precepts and you will be saved." (SDF, p. 2 #3)

Silence alone, of course, does not infuse us with the message from Scripture. It is the prayerfulness and the discipline of Bethlehem that teaches us to read the Scriptures as God's Word and to recognize His presence in our practice of *Lectio Divina*. Bethlehem teaches us to listen trustingly to the Word and to let it fill and strengthen us. During my time at Bethlehem, I have found great comfort from Psalm 131 which advises us to still and quiet our souls like a child at rest in his mother's arms. When we can take that approach, we can relax and let God fill us with His Word. The presence of Christ in the Scripture then comes alive to us in new and deeper ways.

These benefits are particularly important to me since I have not been called to the silence of Bethlehem full time. When I am fed by the bread of the Word at Bethlehem, I am better able to meet Christ in Sacred Scripture when I return to the everyday world. As I once again take up all the tasks for which I am expected to know and to use the Word of God, I can more easily still my soul to receive the Lord, even as I am feeding others on the bread of the Word.

One of the most difficult tasks in our modern world is simply to slow down. We are constantly on the go, and we begin to look at prayer as an interruption or as one more task that we have to accomplish.

When we recognize that we are fed on the bread of the Word, we remember that prayer is more than just an item on the agenda. I often find that when I am distracted or tempted to rush through prayer to get to the next meeting, I can come in silence before God and ask Him to put me back on track. Even if I do not have time for the kind of silence we find at Bethlehem, I find ways to renew that experience. I sometimes find myself simply repeating a phrase from Scripture that reminds me that God is in charge and that I am in His loving presence. I do not dwell on that or on any passage, but I simply let it lead me into quiet before the Lord, Who can then speak to me in the desert of my heart.

Diocesan Priest

The Power of the Word —
Out of Silence and Solitude

Bethlehem keeps me honest. I never realize how unaware of the Lord I become until I spend some time in a hermitage. What amazes me is the simplicity of it. Mostly I sit, silent and alone with the Word, and it happens. I awaken. It's as if I keep falling asleep in the world, and in Bethlehem I keep waking up.

The two lessons that Bethlehem has taught me over the years have been the need for silence and the need for solitude. I would like to say a little about each.

Silence is essential to hear the Word. To hear the Word is to become sensitive to a Presence that is communicative, a Presence that is *speaking* to you. My sensitivity to this Presence is dulled if I'm doing all the talking or if I'm listening to all the voices that normally clamor for my attention. Newspaper headings, billboards, radio, TV, books — even, sometimes, spiritual books — can rush in to fill the silence that should be reserved for God, the silence in which the Presence can be detected. This is why Bethlehem's restriction of reading material to the Scriptures is so wise. I have been in other retreat environments where spiritual reading was available, and I often found myself resorting to it out of a need for distraction, or curiosity, rather than enduring the rigor of a silent vigil with the Word. Hearing the Word does not come easy.

Solitude is essential if the silence is to be complete. We go apart, not only to distance ourselves from the voices of others, but also to confront the many insistent voices we hear within. To let these inner voices jabber away until they are exposed as so many ego-trips. To wait, hopefully, until they drop dead from exhaustion, or at least stop shrieking when they realize no one is paying attention to them. To wait till it is finally quiet. And then, God willing, to hear Him.

> An elder was asked: "What does it mean, this word we read in the Bible, that the way is straight and narrow?" And the elder replied: "This is the straight and narrow way: that a man should do violence to his judgments and cut off, for the love of God, the desires of his own will. This is what was written of the Apostles: 'Behold we have left all things and have followed Thee'." (WD, p. 45 #4)

Bethlehem has been such a wise teacher. The times I have spent in this House of Bread remind me of what Sirach once said of Wisdom: "See for yourselves! I have labored only a little, but have found much."

Cut back on how much television you watch. Your ability to hear the Word will be impaired if you allow the world's words and images indiscriminate access to your consciousness. Check program listings first, and then decide what you will watch, if anything. Be selective. Also, some night, try this: if you happen to catch yourself watching TV in a purely habitual, automatic, and unreflective way, shut it off, open Scripture, and seek the Lord in a deliberate and purposeful manner. How could the Lord not speak to, and be heard by, one who so determinedly turns away from the world's banal chatter in order to pay Him exclusive and undivided attention?

Husband, Father, Parish Deacon, Teacher

Open to God's Voice in Scripture

As a child I had read many lives of the saints who lived in the desert and encountered God in silence and solitude. And so it was no surprise that I had always wanted to make a hermitage retreat.

My retreat took place at the Hermitage of Bethlehem, located in Chester, New Jersey, a lovely wooded area where nature can be seen at its best.

The surroundings were God-filled, silent, peaceful, and inspiring. The sign over the entrance reads: "I will allure her to the desert and speak to her heart" (Ho 2:14).

A close friend of mine had suggested that I take as the theme of my retreat, "My Spirit rejoices in God my Savior, for nothing is impossible to God" (cf. Lk 1:47, 18:27). What a happy coincidence it was when I was assigned to the Hermitage of the Annunciation.

I soon found out that this was a very silent life. At supper time we put our food in a carrier which we used to bring it back to our hermitages. There we were supposed to dine intimately with God. Wherever I turned, I saw words of Scripture; they were on the walls of the hermitage, on the bark of the trees and even on the food carrier itself.

At first the days passed slowly. I loved the absolutely beautiful mornings when I was awakened by an orchestra of birds who sang their songs to the Creator.

The evenings, however, were a little lonely. I felt I needed to hear voices, and all I heard were the sounds of nature which serenaded me to sleep.

The schedule of the retreat was very much my own. The only time we gathered for prayer was in the morning when we would have Mass and Morning Prayer with the hermits.

All prayers were said slowly and meditatively in the spirit of the Desert Fathers. After Communion, we had twenty minutes of contemplative prayer. We had the opportunity of approaching the Sacrament of Reconciliation and of receiving spiritual direction upon request.

On Wednesday, we had our fast day. We received a loaf of bread for the day at a special ceremony after Mass. At the ceremony, we were anointed with oil and urged to listen to the voice of the Lord. On this day, we were allowed to spend only one hour alone in the chapel; the rest of the day was spent in the hermitage and around the grounds.

On Thursday, we had Solemn Vespers. The Blessed Sacrament was exposed for three hours daily and we were free to choose the hour we wanted; however, many of the retreatants spent more than the chosen hour.

The chapel was quiet and conducive to prayer. The only book we were encouraged to read was the Bible. In the hermitages there were guides on how to read the Bible, meditate and contemplate God. I discovered that God's Word acquires a deeper meaning in silence and solitude.

St. Epiphanius said: "To know nothing of the divine law is a betrayal of salvation." St. Anthony the Great said: "You have heard Scripture. That should teach you how to be saved." (JWD, p. 108)

As the retreat was about to end, I felt a surge of gratitude welling up within me for the opportunity of coming to behold God face to face. This retreat was a *peak experience of my religious life*, one I will not easily forget.

As I locked my hermitage door and took one last look at this *meeting tent with the Almighty*, I found myself talking to Bethlehem.

Bethlehem, I've learned so much from you. I've learned that silence and solitude are good companions. I've learned to be open to God's voice, especially in Scripture, and that happiness can only be found in God alone.

Salesian Sister

Entering the Mystery of the Word at Bethlehem

The Word of God contains the self-disclosure of the life-creating Trinity and is the soul of all true theology — knowledge of God. In many and varied ways throughout Scripture the Triune God makes Himself known so that He may love and be loved more fully, for who can love another fully unless there is a deep knowledge of the other's mysterious interior life? In this Word He made known not only His love for us, but an even greater mystery: He longs to be longed for, loves to be loved and desires to be desired. It is into this great truth that God's Word leads us.

At Bethlehem, the Word of God is a central focus, broken together with the Bread of Life at every liturgy. At Bethlehem the language spoken is the language of the Spirit which can only be heard in the Womb of silence and solitude. It is a hearing of the heart and it is in the heart that the Father utters a word which knows no bounds, contained only by His life-giving Breath. It is a hearing which begins with the written word entering the mind and ends with the mind's descent into the silent temple of the heart. In this hermitage of the heart the vision of Isaiah is contained, and only there do we encounter the thrice-holy Mystery who took flesh in the Virgin's womb. To this place the Word must lead us, for just as Mary was only able to conceive the Word after receiving and accepting the Word of God from the angel in her *fiat*, so must we incessantly read God's Word, listen and respond in a life of service to the Gospel of Christ. Only by doing the Father's will, revealed in Scripture, will we be able to give birth to Jesus every day in our lives and become Bread broken and offered for the life of the world.

If we are to enter into this deep relationship of love with God and live all of the demands of the Gospel, we must take seriously the call to listen daily to His Word in Scripture. Whether you decide to follow the Church's cycle of readings, or to simply take a passage from the Old or New Testament, make it a habit and set quiet time aside every day — even if it is only for a few minutes — and let the Spirit speak to your heart through the words He inspired. I am only able to find quiet time for *lectio* in the early morning. I usually take a few verses, meditate simply on their meaning, allow them to work within me and end with prayer. The Father will reward you for your effort and will transform you into the image of His Son by the working of the Holy Spirit.

May the Spirit use these simple words to awaken within you a love for the Word, who desires only to lead you to His Father. Amen.

Seminarian

You Belong to Me

I was scheduled for Eucharistic Adoration. I planned to divide the hour into three parts. I would read the psalms; I would do centering prayer; I told myself to let God do what He would with the final part.

Seated at the back of the chapel, I began to read the psalms. I was alone and felt quite at ease and comfortable. After finishing my readings, I moved to the front of the chapel, where the Blessed Sacrament was exposed.

I settled into a kneeling position directly in front of the Host. As I gazed at it, I distinctly received this message:

"You belong to me, John.
You really do.
I will never let you go."

These were words without sound. They reverberated within me. They still do in my heart. For me they were the echo of the Lord Jesus' words in the Gospel of Matthew: "I am always with you" (Mt 28:20).

The geography of God locates us properly in His presence. Through Jesus — Word made Bread — we are present to the God Who loves us. A frequent practice of spending even ten minutes before the Lord Jesus would balance our posture. If we are unable to visit a

51

church, we could use a crucifix or a picture to be simply present to the Lord. His silent yet strong presence to us is a key to unlock for us the door to life. To be open to Him in our minds and hearts is a great gift that should be used simply yet frequently. Our silent presence to Jesus assures us of His strong presence in our lives

Diocesan Priest

Eucharist — Unseen but Felt

Each of the many times I have been on retreat at Bethlehem has always been a very unique experience. Days ahead I find myself anticipating, praying and preparing for the graces the Lord has in store for me during this time of solitude and prayer.

Like all retreatants I come tired and pressured from ministry. Yet, turning into Tony's Road is both a quickening and a quieting and a readiness to begin launching *out*, better yet, *in*.

I am a Dominican with a Franciscan love of nature so the pine forest sings and breathes God to me, while the sparseness and simplicity of the hermitage help me to unwind as I await my visitations.

Key for me, though, is the daily Eucharistic Liturgy during my sojourn at Bethlehem. My community liturgies are beautifully prepared and satisfying. Jubilee and community assemblies are inspiring and energizing so I'm not spiritually undernourished, yet at Bethlehem something unseen but felt happens. Perhaps like the *cloud* of Old Testament times, one feels led and in a sense enveloped and bonded with the hermits and those of us who have gathered to witness again the unfathomable mystery of the undying gift of Redemption and to hear with more awareness: "Grant that we who are nourished by His body and blood may be filled with the Holy Spirit and become one body and one spirit in Christ. . . and may He make of us an everlasting gift to You." Truly Jesus and His invisible world are present when in the awesomeness of Consecration, the miracle of Transubstantiation happens among us. Personally, I hear the silence and the sacredness of the moment. Another plus of the liturgy is the extended time after Holy Communion; to stay and be with the Lord. No deadlines to be met, no need to hurry out.

Eucharistic moments at the daily Holy Hour are for me an extension of the graces of the morning's Eucharist, especially on Desert Day when one is totally alone with Jesus; I found I can even sing to Him.

My Bethlehem experience of Eucharist! How does one really pen it? In the world of hermits and hermitages my love of the Eucharist has been enriched and enlivened with an increased sense of the awesomeness of the mystery and the Father's love.

Summing up my hermitage experience with its simplicity of lifestyle in a consumer society reinforces a Japanese proverb for me: "WABI SABI: less is more."

Caldwell Dominican Sister

In the Heart of the Host

I have made many retreats in my life; ten of them at Bethlehem in Chester. On each return I have found myself *at home*. Here I have, in the words of the poet Gerard Manley Hopkins, "fled with a fling of the heart to the heart of the Host." The profound joy of the daily shared Eucharistic celebration is extended each afternoon in solitary Eucharistic adoration. I meet God in the hospitality of the house, in the humble hermitage, in hearing the Word of God and most particularly in the simple chapel in *the heart of the Host*.

A busy, active, noisy, cluttered, teen-age apostolate sends me to my knees often to cry out to touch God with the needs of the work and of the people I love and serve. At Bethlehem, in the chapel, before the tabernacle, I have touched God and been touched by God. I have come *home* and recognized the Voice saying, "Make your home in Me." With Augustine "I believe, so that I may understand." Spending time before the Blessed Sacrament I have come to understand Archbishop Fulton J. Sheen's advice to make the Holy Hour daily — to tell God your story and to hear the reply. And I have come to know why Cornelia Connelly, our foundress, "habitually sought the Lord in the Blessed Sacrament" and "taught a strong eucharistic piety." At the Bethlehem Hermitage I have been able to drink deeply of the heritage of this devotion which has, since childhood, been food for my spirit. I thank God for this Gift Incarnate in Bethlehem of Judea and in Bethlehem of Chester, New Jersey.

It has been said that given the choice to hear a lecture *about* God in one room or to spend time *with* God in the next room, most of us would choose the lecture. If this is true — what a loss! To prefer to hear about Him rather than to hear Him. Are we busy, blind, afraid, awed or just stupid? "When we see the invisible, we can do the impossible," wrote Archbishop Sheen. So, in the spirit of Bethlehem one does well to sometimes choose a church visit over a companionable chat, or an evening of recollection over an evening at a restaurant. How does a busy doctor, a tired patient, a harried mother, an overworked father, a person pulled from pillar to post by family, friends, work, obligations find time for self, for spiritual refreshment? Steal moments of silence to make a visit to the Blessed Sacrament, at least in spirit. Remember that the hermits of Bethlehem are *sentinels of adoration and burning love* before the Blessed Sacrament and unite yourself in spirit with them. Unable to be physically before the tabernacle, be in the remembrance of that Presence and use the Word of God in Scripture to bring you to the Lord. Let Bethlehem be in your heart and on your mind and with the earnest intention to be with Him. Soon you will find yourself seeking the Lord in the Blessed Sacrament — source of life and love.

Sister of the Holy Child Jesus

Eucharist — Primary Importance

Bethlehem, with its strong Eucharistic emphasis, helps to remind anyone who journeys there that the Real Presence of Jesus in the Eucharist is of primary importance. The routine of daily activity can become sterile as we perform our duties day in and day out. In the area of religious duties — going to church, teaching religious education, being faithful to prayer, etc. — we can begin to simply perform them by rote. Being creatures of habit, we can lose focus of the essential and fall into a pattern of mechanically performing the rites of religion by rote, void of their essential meaning.

Bethlehem helps me to return to the essentials and to rediscover them in a new and wonderful way. Everything about Bethlehem is directed to the Eucharistic Lord. Bethlehem is true to its name, for it truly is the place or house of Bread. For the Bethlehemite, the bread of Eucharist is truly Jesus. Jesus is God, and God is the most important thing in life. God is the meaning of who I can become; without Him there is no meaning to life, no purpose to live.

Bethlehem is the place we need to come to as often as we can so that we can readjust our bearings on what is truly important. When life in the marketplace becomes hectic and complex, the Eucharist reminds me that it is in the simple things that God is to be found. God uses simple things: bread, water and wine to remind us that His presence is to be found among the simple in society. The Eucharist tells me in my solitude that God's way of revealing Himself has not changed all that much from the way He first revealed Himself at Bethlehem.

The practicalities of the Eucharist are many, but for me there has been one practicality which I have often reflected upon and which continues to have great impact on my life as a priest. The Eucharist, when I view it in the Mass and especially when I receive it, reminds me of the presence of Christ in me. The reception of the Holy Eucharist not only helps me to remember that Christ lives in me, but it enables me to penetrate deeper into that mystical reality. My solitude at Bethlehem has taught me that Eucharist is truly "Emmanuel" or "God with us" in the active events that life places before us. This conviction which Jesus offers to us as grace enables the Christian to view reality from the vantage point of Christian hope. The virtue of hope tells us that all the events of our life, the good as well as the bad, have buried within them the seeds which eventually blossom and bring us to the Kingdom of God.

Diocesan Priest, Washington, D.C.

To Adore the Eucharist:
Essence of My Priesthood and
Our Christian Life

During my visits to the hermitage at Bethlehem, I have acquired a deeper appreciation of Eucharistic contemplation in the midst of an active life as a Franciscan parish priest. I understand my Franciscan spirituality as a call to the contemplative dimension within an active ministerial life.

The hermitage is not only a haven of peace, but an anchor for the spiritual journey. The hermitage is not simply a place to go to get away; it slowly becomes a powerful symbol, to remind me that I must walk in the footsteps of Jesus and go into the quiet wilderness to face my temptations and hear the voice of God anew. Therefore, the hermitage becomes integral to the Christian life where I must be constantly converted into a *house of bread* for others.

In the stillness of Bethlehem, one can feel the sunshine warming a frosty leaf and taste the raindrops caught in a delicate spider web. Surrounded by God's creatures, the Holy Spirit visits the one who prays and opens his or her heart to God without pretense. United to the Eucharistic Lord, one is challenged by the probing yet gentle Spirit of God to become holy as God is holy.

The quiet hermitage at Bethlehem has helped me to sing anew St. Francis' Canticle of Creatures. Following his example, all of God's creatures lead me to adore the Eucharistic Lord perhaps as never before. To adore the Eucharist surrounded by the beauties of nature challenges me to reflect God's love and presence infinitely more than all creatures together.

The Eucharist was a source of deep solace to the monks in the midst of their struggles, and Abba Poemen reminded his listeners of this with a colorful interpretation of one of the Psalms. Poemen cites Ps 42:1, "As the deer longs for flowing streams, so my soul longs for You, my God."

He then suggests that the monks are like those deer in that they "are burned by the venom of evil demons, and they long for Saturday and Sunday to come to be able to go to the springs of water, that is to say, the body and blood of the Lord, so as to be purified from the bitterness of the evil one." (JWD, p. 201)

To adore the Eucharist reminds me that the simple Bread held in suspension and worshipped in contemplation is the same God I hold at every consecration. The words of St. Augustine challenge us: "See what you are and become what you see, the body of Christ." So do the words of St. Clare of Assisi in her second letter to Blessed Agnes of Prague: "Gaze upon Him, consider Him, contemplate Him as you desire to imitate Him." To adore the Eucharist is to become Christlike; humble, servant and bread for others which is the essence of my priesthood and our Christian life.

The hermitage experience helps one to integrate peace, quiet contemplation and spiritual insight into one's everyday life. To experience the Eucharist as a separate entity without seeing its profound impact on one's entire life is to miss its *hidden manna*.

Applying the fruits of contemplation to an active Christian life is a constant challenge. Here are a few practical suggestions:

— Pray 15-20 minutes a day in a quiet place where there are no distractions. Praying before or after celebrating the Eucharist is particularly beneficial.

— Read and pray the Sacred Scriptures at the beginning or end of your active day. Reflect on the Scriptures proclaimed for the Mass of the day. Reflect on the mysteries you celebrate in the sacraments and apply your joys and sufferings to Christ as you receive Him in the Eucharist and contemplate Him in the Gospels.

— A symbolic prayer gesture is one that is laden with meaning. For example, to prostrate myself before the Eucharist at the hermitage powerfully reminds me of my ordination. Every time I do this at home or in the church, I remember my consecration and recommit myself to God anew.

With this powerful posture, I reenact the hermitage experience and that of ordination. Each time, my prayer and ministry are added to it. It becomes an incarnational prayer which summarizes and sanctifies my entire life! You may have other symbolic prayer postures that are meaningful for you. Integrate them into your prayer experiences.

Although not exhaustive, I am confident these suggestions foster a discipline of prayer within an active life and will gently form you into Bethlehem, a *house of God's living Bread* for others.

Franciscan Priest, O.F.M.

Mary, Mother of the Word

There can be no Bethlehem without Mary. She was the instrument used by the Lord to give flesh to the Word. That was the Bethlehem of our salvation history 2000 years ago. However, the Bethlehem of Chester, New Jersey, in my experience from many retreats spent there and from knowing many who have made retreats there, proves to be just as true. The Mother of the Lord is central to any experience at the Bethlehem Hermitage. She continues to give flesh to the Word for all who seek that Word in the desert experience provided by the hermitage. In the very name of Bethlehem, the house of bread, the bread of the Word and Eucharist shine forth as the main vehicles of grace at that blessed place.

Bethlehem Hermitage helped me to focus especially on Mary, as the Mother of the Word. I was able to listen and to be open to the Word because of the blessed silence and solitude. I made certain that I would only take the Word with me into the hermitage even though at times it was very difficult; it was then that I was able to come to terms with myself and what the Lord was asking of me. I really felt the power and challenge of the Word in those moments. It was then that I would go to Mary and seek her help and intercession. Her icon graced my hermitage and when I would go to the chapel, again her icon would make her presence felt in a very real way. That was when I realized so strongly that there could be no real Bethlehem without Mary. Yes, even in Chester, New Jersey.

> Once, Abba Isaac came upon Poemen while he was caught up "in ecstasy." He was so struck by what he saw, that he threw himself before Poemen and begged him, "Tell me where you were." Poemen said, "My thought was there, where holy Mary, the Mother of God stood and wept near the cross of the Savior (Jn 19:25)." Poemen acknowledged that it was the example of her tears which stood out for him above all else: "I wish I could always weep like that."
>
> (JWD, p. 189)

The real success of any retreat is always known several weeks after the retreat, when one has settled down into the ordinary routine of life. Then one can remember the graces and insights given during the retreat. I knew from experience that I had to take Bethlehem with me into my work and into my people, in my case, the seminarians. Mary of Bethlehem came into a new perspective, for now she had to be the Mary of wherever or whatever in my daily life and work for the Church, especially at the seminary. In my silent prayer which grew stronger in the atmosphere of Bethlehem, I was able to wait on the Word and then celebrate it with my people during the Eucharist. I was able to do this through the intercession of Mary as I prepared for my daily Mass. Mary became the center of my life as a priest, and was felt in all that I did. That is why I need to go back to that sacred desert and meet God in His Word and with His Mother. I have continually encouraged my seminarians, especially those under my direction, to experience at least once in their time at the seminary, the desert provided by Bethlehem and the good hermits who live there.

Seminarians of the past, who are now priests, have never ceased to praise and remember with gratitude their experience at Bethlehem. For this we thank our good God. I still take seminarians for their retreat there and I can see the good effects in their lives, a deepening of the life of prayer through centering which is provided for by the very atmosphere of Bethlehem, and a deepening of their love for the Word. That Word which they spend so many hours studying, they come to feel in prayer through the silence and solitude.

Another effect of their retreat at Bethlehem is a deepening of their love and devotion to our Blessed Mother. Devotion to her is central in the life of a priest. She brings us, her priestly sons, closer to her Son the great High Priest. Bethlehem provides this so beautifully. The ending of the day with the singing of the Salve Regina as we gaze on the beautiful icon of Mary of Bethlehem especially touches me and all those who make a retreat there. How well I remember those special moments when all seemed so simple and possible through her wonderful intercession.

Yes, there can be no real Bethlehem without the Mother of the Word. May all who come to Bethlehem drink of the waters of the Word and of the Blessed Eucharist. For me there is no other place like it on earth.

The Word of God must become our daily bread. I would suggest that one resolution to bring from the retreat is to read and ponder the Word daily for a few quiet moments. In this way, each day will have its moment of desert, of hermitage, of Bethlehem.

Diocesan Priest, Spiritual Director, Pastor

Learning from Mary

Mary did not have absolute certitude about God's plan in her life. But she had a deep trust that whatever God wanted was best for her. Her confidence in Him grew as she "treasured all these things and pondered them in her heart" (Lk 2:19).

My time at Bethlehem provides an intense period of focusing on the Lord, learning deeper trust in His all-loving Providence. This is a treasure that comes with me when I leave Bethlehem to return to my regular duties. I believe God wishes me to trust Him completely, radically. I have learned so much of this from Mary.

The Rule of the Hermits of Bethlehem (published by Alba House as *A Way of Desert Spirituality*) mentions the miracle at Cana to show how Mary ". . . proclaim[s] the Word not only by. . . speech, but by. . . actions and attitudes." Mary makes no request, only a statement: "They have no wine." Jesus seems unwilling to do anything about it. But I believe there is a level of communication between Mother and Son no words can express. So she can say, "Do whatever He tells you," and be confident of the outcome. It is silence and contemplation that enables one to be increasingly united to the will of God.

We are, in a sense, all called to a hermitage existence. No matter how *busy* life becomes, God wants us to retreat, however briefly, into that sanctuary within where He alone dwells. Mary pondered the Word even in the midst of life's duties. We are able to imitate this because a moment's loving attentiveness to His Presence is a powerful act of love.

Each of us needs increasing awareness of the *God within* to learn how much He loves us and to lead us to a deeper appreciation of every person's worth, most especially, those we find hard to like. He teaches us we can love without liking.

Sister of Charity, New York

Spiritual Direction

In the Eastern tradition it is the role of the Spiritual Father or Mother to act as a guide, someone who points the way to the experience of the Ultimate Reality, God. The disciple looks to the guide and gazes with the guide in the direction to which the finger points.

One pitfall in this relationship can occur when the disciple focuses only with his or her eye on the *finger* and not beyond it. It would be as if a sailor became totally enthralled with the compass on the ship, and never moved beyond the harbor, away from which the compass leads.

The role, then, of the Spiritual Director must be one of an exquisite transparency. This person must mirror the grace of the Holy Spirit with a clarity and openness that envelops the disciple in a vision that leads to an internal experience of the Father and His loving will in one's life. To focus on anything else could create an obstacle in the disciple's journey towards Uncreated Love.

The Spiritual Director is also not a problem solver for the directee. The journey begun is a mystery to be lived out in a sincere seeking of the Father's Will. The Spiritual Director must be a person of prayer and discernment, who enables the directee to *see* for himself or herself this Mystery of God's beckoning Presence in their life. The inevitable sufferings and trials in this journey are open to the scrutiny and discernment of the Spiritual Director in such a way that the unfolding of the Mystery enables the directee, with his or her help, towards an identification with the Paschal Mystery of Christ.

The revelations to be experienced in this relationship with the Holy Spirit are best found in the framework of Holy Scripture that is prayed and pursued in an atmosphere of silence and solitude. It is necessary for the directee to give a certain amount of daily time to prayer and Scripture study.

I have come to these conclusions from my actual experience of retreats and being under spiritual guidance at Bethlehem Hermitage. This has enabled me to face the sufferings and trials in my life with loving support from people of prayer. My personal discouragement, and sometimes anger, has been accepted and transformed into an opportunity to see God's will in my life as a strengthening and healing gift. This has come through my own prayerful silence and solitude with Sacred Scripture, and under the faith-filled direction I have received at Bethlehem Hermitage. I have been helped to discern the face of Jesus in the situations in my life, and to recognize my personal invitation into His Paschal Mystery.

Wife, Mother, Spiritual Director

Attuned to the Spirit

Anyone wishing to experience the life of a Bethlehem Hermit for a weekend or a week is welcome. The prayer of silence and solitude becomes an effective door to the healing presence of God in this physical and spiritual environment. An atmosphere of prayer is our gift to our guests. In the spirit of the desert the Sacrament of Reconciliation is provided and the opportunity for spiritual direction when the Desert Father is available.

— Brochure describing the Bethlehem Experience

The emphasis of a week or weekend at Bethlehem is on prayer and silence. Immersed in this atmosphere, there is a gradual winding down from the bustle of ordinary routine. Then sets in a period of waiting, of listening.

From experience, Our Lord speaks in some way to the retreatant through nature, through Scripture, through the morning's homily. And this word weaves itself into the prayer and silence of the week, offering a message to the individual.

It is usually at the end of my stay at Bethlehem that I have brought this word for confirmation to the table of reconciliation and spiritual direction. This is where the actions of my daily life are examined and joined to the fruit of the week's prayer. There is an atmosphere of freedom at this meeting, knowing that: "The spiritual father enables the disciple to see oneself as one truly is and assists the person in discovering the truth for oneself. . . He does this, not by teaching his own way, but by instructing the disciple to find the proper way oneself. He acts as God's usher and is not the main character. All the desert father does is meant to guide and direct the disciple to God" (*A Way of Desert Spirituality*, p. 60).

> *Abba Antony said, "The man who abides in solitude and is quiet, is delivered from fighting three battles — those of hearing, speech and sight. Then he will have but one battle to fight — the battle of the heart."* (WA, p. 40, #2)

There are many styles of spiritual direction available today. When one comes to Bethlehem, it is with the realization that no formal outline is first produced into which must be worked the prayer of the week. "There is responsibility on the part of both the desert father and the disciple. They both must be praying to be in touch with the Holy Spirit because truly it is the Holy Spirit who guides the soul" (ibid., p. 61). The end step in the process is to look together at the workings of the Spirit, and hopefully, to grow in love and adoration of the Triune God.

Dominican Sister, Amityville, New York

Unburdening and Liberation

During my days at Bethlehem, the words of Scripture, the power of memory and the fruitfulness of the natural world all worked together. I had a vivid awareness of my sins and a renewed experience of the unburdening and liberation of the Sacrament of Penance. The idols against which Moses contended, *the useless things*, reminded me of my own addictions and sins which kept me from approaching the Lord with a *pure heart* and *face to face*. Painful memories of my own past offenses made me question over and over how to undo the damage I had done to myself, to others and to God.

> *A brother sinned and the priest ordered him to go out of the church; Abba Bessarion got up and went out with him, saying, "I, too, am a sinner."*
> (DRDF, p. 25)

The beginning of an answer, the hint of an explanation, came with the observation, everywhere around me, of luxuriant new growth arising from and transforming old and dead tree trunks and limbs. There was indeed nothing I could do to make amends or to deserve forgiveness. Only the love of Jesus, and His blood shed for me, could provide the water for new growth and make useful and beautiful new things spring up from the barren field of my life. After confession, I felt for a while, an uncanny sense of being in an earthly paradise.

To try and preserve this experience beyond a written record, I resolved to take a concrete element from the Bethlehem Hermitage where the grace was given and insert it into the environment of my everyday life. I literally transplanted a tiny pine sapling from Bethlehem to a garden at home. It is a living reminder and a direct link with the new experience of Penance I had at Bethlehem: growth, freedom and a feeling of beginning again.

Jesuit Priest

Reconciliation and the Desert Experience

My desert experience began at Bethlehem in November of 1977. It came at a time when I was very much immersed in the material world. I was successful in business, had a wonderful and supportive wife and two beautiful and healthy children. Everything seemed to be going well on the surface. However, my spiritual life was far from good, even though at the time I didn't realize it.

So I went to Bethlehem for what I supposed was going to be a regular directed retreat. I was welcomed and greeted warmly and led into the woods to my lodging, a hermitage. At this point the routines at Bethlehem were explained to me and I was left on my own with my Bible and God. This was not going to be just another retreat!

After many hours of meditation and some contemplation, I met with the Desert Father and described my situation. At that time I explained that I was praying for a change in my occupation so that I could become a better person. The Desert Father just listened and then gave me three or four readings to meditate on. For one and a half days that's all I did, and then I decided to take a walk and to say the rosary. It was during that walk that I received my answer. God made it very clear to me that He didn't want me to change jobs but wanted me to stay right where I was. It also became clear to me that no matter what you do for a living, you have to always be aware of God's presence within you and bring Him with you whatever you're doing.

> *A soldier asked Abba Mios if God accepted repentance. After the old man had taught him many things, he said, "Tell me, my dear, if your cloak is torn, do you throw it away?" He replied, "No, I mend it and use it again." The old man said to him, "If you are so careful about your cloak, will not God be equally careful about his creature?"* (DRDF, p. 51)

Later, I shared what had happened with the Desert Father, expecting him to be surprised. However, he just smiled and nodded his head as if he knew that it was going to happen. At this time, I received the Sacrament of Reconciliation in a way that I had never experienced before. I felt an assurance of God's forgiveness and of His mercy, and truly felt that this was a new beginning. The overwhelming experience of God's loving mercy was both humbling and joyfully freeing. Since that time, I have continued to return to Bethlehem and the Desert Father for the Sacrament of Reconciliation.

Going to town one day to sell some small articles, Abba Agathon met a cripple on the roadside, paralyzed in his legs, who asked him where he was going. Abba Agathon replied, "To town, to sell some things." The other said, "Do me the favor of carrying me there." So he carried him to the town. The cripple said to him, "Put me down where you sell your wares." He did so. When he had sold an article, the cripple asked, "What did you sell it for?" and he told him the price. The other said, "Buy me a cake," and he bought it. When Abba Agathon had sold a second article, the sick man asked, "How much did you sell it for?" And he told him the price of it. Then the other said, "Buy me this," and he bought it. When Agathon, having sold all his wares, wanted to go, he said to him, "Are you going back?" and he replied, "Yes." Then said he, "Do me the favor of carrying me back to the place where you found me." Once more picking him up, he carried him back to that place. Then the cripple said, "Agathon, you are filled with divine blessings, in heaven and on earth." Raising his eyes, Agathon saw no man. It was an angel of the Lord, come to try him. (SDF, p. 25, #30)

To practically apply the message of Bethlehem, there are certain daily steps that I follow. Each day I start off with Mass and the Eucharist, the Bread of Life. After Mass I try to say a rosary and then — most importantly — sometime during the day, usually early afternoon, I take ten minutes away from the routine to just be in His presence. This is both a time to listen and to check out your progress for the day. At the end of the day, a daily examen is also helpful to see where you've either failed or progressed toward God.

Husband, Father

67

Pierced by God's Love

Bethlehem has been for me a special place of encounter with the Lord for many years. Each desert experience has been a time of emptying and healing. I have come each summer with great expectations and have never been disappointed. Through these many desert encounters I have experienced the Lord's presence in many ways; perhaps the most outstanding being an intense awareness of His healing love in the Sacrament of Reconciliation.

How often before coming to Bethlehem I had tried *to do better* with little or no success. On one occasion while reflecting on the Parables of Mercy, a new sense of freedom was given to me. Recalling that in my early formation great value was placed on the concept of compunction, I realized that I had never really internalized the meaning of the term. During this time of reflection, however, I became aware of what it means to be touched or pierced by God's love. Since that experience, each reception of the Sacrament of Reconciliation has become more meaningful in my life. I know now that it is God's reconciling love that empowers me to nourish mutual healing, to foster reconciliation and to move towards closer union with God and neighbor.

Sister of St. Joseph, Chestnut Hill, PA

Confronting the False Self

Know Thyself! These words above the entrance to the Delphic Oracle in Greece convey the promise and hope of modern psychology. Yet many wear the mask of false self, avoiding self-discovery at every turn. Thus our unconscious programs for happiness, in place by age 3-4, go undetected although they profoundly influence our adult choices. When, for example, our childish expectation for security is frustrated, we can experience anger, jealousy and grief. Unchallenged, these lead to resistance to change, fossilizing into programs for happiness that can never deliver.

We counter this by changing the direction of our search for happiness, and by being open to self-knowledge. This effort, which can lead to transforming union, is helped when we make psychology the handmaid of theology.

When the afflictive emotions are triggered by frustration of instinctual needs and by the unconscious value system, we are confronted by negative feelings best coped with through regular contemplative prayer. Where problems are severe, psychotherapy may be indicated. We challenge the old emotional programs and their beliefs. This can lead to conscious resolve to change. Thus if I insist others *must* treat me better, I dispute this irrational belief, replacing it with more realistic preferences: "Yes, ideally John would relate to me better, but it's not the end of the world if he doesn't." This results in greater interior freedom and better response to the needs and personalities of others. As we think so we feel, and both of these affect our physiological responses.

> *Plotinus claims that "each of us is an intellectual cosmos," that the journey of the soul is "a voyage of self-discovery.... If we wish to know the Real, we have only to look within ourselves."*
>
> (JWD, p. 52)

At Bethlehem I was able for the first time to devote enough time to prayer so that in seeking God there, I allowed myself to be found by Him. And I started to better understand the nature of the false self.

Obviously, a hermitage is not the only place where this happens. But in the world it is typically more difficult. A major challenge for me was to create my own desert in the midst of a busy life. Not a place of escape but of conversion from the false to the new and authentic self. This required the self-discipline to set aside sufficient time and proper place. My ongoing challenge is to bring the fruits of solitude back to others, so that spirituality and service blend together.

In the words of Theophane the Recluse, renowned Russian Orthodox spiritual guide, "It is inner work which gives to all our external activities their purpose and effectiveness."

Husband, Father, Permanent Deacon, Psychologist

A Battle for the Mind

There were, no doubt, various winds that drove men and women into the desert. One driving wind which must have whirled down the corridor of the two centuries of persecution, underground faith, and catacomb-spirituality, was Saint Paul's "tornado" admonition: "Do not conform yourselves to this age but be transformed by the renewal of your mind" (Rm 12:2). He meant it for the early Christians surrounded by the mind-set of glorious and pagan Rome.

After the great triumph of the Edict of Milan (325 A.D.), Christianity became public. It also became powerful, sophisticated, rich and noisy. The Desert Mothers and Fathers of the Christian Roman Empire heard Saint Paul's call as well, and fled the cities and towns. And so it goes — down the centuries. The worldly mind-set is in competition with the Gospel, and usually winning.

Today is no different. The priest today is found in a cacophony of noise, programs, projects, and activities. There is a subtle, but still apparent, persecution of the Church from without and within her walls. Our mind-sets wrestle with secular thinking on everything from music videos to life-support; they grappled over life-issues such as abortion, artificial contraception, assisted suicide, unassisted suicide, and the scary potential of technological eugenics. It all boggles the mind. It's still a battle for the mind. That hasn't changed since Adam and Eve tuned in the Serpent and listened to his commercial on the apple — and they bought it. They wanted to *know* good and evil.

Every temptation begins in the mind. If the Evil One can get into your mind, he has his ugly foot in the door. And the mind is besieged all day long with noises — and Saint Paul keeps telling us "renew your mind. . . change the way you *think*."

The first Desert Fathers knew that what you put into your mind matters. This is the principle behind *lectio divina* and prayer. Holy leisure has an end. To fill the mind with God's words, psalms, hymns, and sacred reading, will have an effect on the way one thinks and acts and reacts to life. Unfortunately this "holy leisure" is not on the schedule or agenda (even hidden) for many, if not most priests, or so I thought until I discovered the best kept secret in north New Jersey — the little Hermitage of Bethlehem!

I arrived on a Sunday afternoon — filled with the noise of the Sabbath still ringing in my ears: homilies and tired hymns — themselves soothing the inner-noise stirred up from driving across Manhattan and through the Lincoln Tunnel. Unloading my car of its single bag was easy. Unloading my mind of the accumulated stimulation took days. Alone in my assigned hermitage on the edge of the woods, there was no television, radio, telephone (thank you, Jesus) or newspaper. No fax, no traffic outside, and no people making people-noises. There was no grand selection of spiritually stimulating books or newspapers, just the Scriptures.

My hermitage was named "Most Holy Trinity." It was quite comfortable in its stark simplicity. No cave, but a wood-pine cabin with hard wood floor and mouse-proof siding. It had a corner oratory where hung an icon of Rublev's Trinity over a bare wooden altar, and an unpadded prie-dieu. There was a twin size bed with a firm mattress on a wooden platform, a writing/eating table, and a small rocking chair. And, yes, I had all the creature-needs available: a private bathroom with shower.

I think there may have been angels there, too, as something prompted me to pray compline in my oratory — out loud. I don't often hear that voice.

There is for me a solemnness about the early hours before dawn — especially when away on retreat. To have the leisure to read slowly the Office of Readings and actually *think* about the psalms or that Old Testament excerpt or to pray over the Mass readings for the day. I don't always get up on time to enjoy such luxury. My first retreat resolution: "Get up earlier to read and pray." The mind is renewable early in the morning (after a cup of coffee) before it becomes the sponge of the day's noise. Early morning silence is too easily raped by radio news and the sound of music.

The day goes by quite quickly, and I find myself sitting at the wide window watching the sun go down and the deer disperse to wherever they go, as sleep comes easier (after compline) than the night before.

On Wednesdays the permanent hermits and we temporary hermits have a "desert day." After morning Mass, Father blesses a large basket of bread neatly packed in plastic bags. He prays over each person and "anoints" each one's forehead (the mind!) with oil to strengthen us for a day of special solitude and fasting. We are blessed, given our daily bread, and disperse to our hermitages like deer at sundown. Each temporary hermit, not having the Blessed Sacrament in the private oratory as the permanent hermits do, signs up (last night) for an hour of solitary adoration in the chapel. NO regular meals are served, no silent meal lines like the last three days when we've gotten to know each other without the use of words. Just bread. . . good, hearty, homemade bread.

I appreciated this Wednesday bread-fast, especially at Thursday's break-fast, when I had both prayer and lunch to look forward to. This is the fifth day, and by now much of the worldly stimulation has left me. The mind is calmer and somehow more receptive to prayer. The steady aloneness doesn't signal "dissipation" but a quiet conscious-ness of God's presence within you. We know it and preach about it, but aren't always too aware of it.

Bethlehem has miles of woods to walk in. Being so close to nature renews the mind and the spirit, re-minding me how deprived I am of this reality when my nature-trails are asphalt highways and city streets; car horns and yellow cabs don't raise my mind and heart to the Creator like bird calls and fat groundhogs do. How many shades of green are seen in the afternoon sunlight caught in the trees! Every day becomes centered on the sunburst caught in the tabernacle doorway of the quiet, rustic chapel. The hour or more of adoration before the Lord in the Eucharist adds a whole new depth to one's day.

Priestly priorities. What is a priest, if not a man of and for the Eucharist? This is my whole life. The Sacrifice I offer every day in the person of Christ is the most important "thing" I do. Where is the source of my strength, the meaning of my ministry and the cause of my joy, if not the Eucharist? Everything else takes on a different color when viewed in its hues. My thinking is off when "saying Mass" is just another function among a multiplicity of ministries. This is why I was ordained. This and the Sacrament of Reconciliation, are the heart of my "being a priest" after the heart of Jesus, the Priest.

When this goes, my thinking gets off the track. When I "think" of these as burdens or obligations or functions or one ministry among many — then I am in trouble. I look to people, projects, accomplishments, compliments, and creature comforts to give "meaning" to my priestly life. If I forget that I am made by Love Eternal — *for* Love Eternal — and forget that Jesus in the Blessed Sacrament is the Source and End of my loving, then I begin to "think" that other people, places and finite things are going to satisfy that infinite desire in me. When I think and act as if this passing world will make me happy, my thinking needs to be renewed. I've conformed myself to this present age too much, and have put on the mind of the world, and not the mind of Christ, not the mind of His Church.

Being at Bethlehem, this "house of bread," one begins to realize that the Lord dwells among us in the Eucharist and this is the heart of these permanent hermits' whole life. From their Rule of Life we read:

"Eucharistic Adoration is the extension of the Eucharistic Sacrifice. In the name of the Church, the hermit is a sentinel of adoration and burning love. The hermit's poor prayer is immersed in the Eucharistic Heart of Jesus and is led by the Holy Spirit to offer adoration, thanksgiving, praise, reparation and intercession before our Heavenly Father on behalf of the Church Universal. We pray particularly for our Holy Father, the Bishop of Paterson, all Bishops, Priests, Deacons, Seminarians and Religious. Our prayerful concern, too, is for the sanctity and unity of family life and for those who do not know

Christ and all the people of God." (*A Way of Desert Spirituality: The Rule of Life of the Hermits of Bethlehem of the Heart of Jesus*, New York: Alba House, 1992, p. 22).

If our priestly minds are going to be renewed and less and less conformed to this present age, we need to flee to more deserts and less desserts. We need to discover ourselves in the sacrament and sacrifice of Love. We can only be transformed "through Him, with Him and in Him."

The Bethlehem Hermits in the Heart of Jesus live in the heart of the Church. Only there can we screw our heads on straight and be renewed for battle. If I may slightly distort the words of Saint Augustine, "Our *minds* are restless, O Lord, until they rest in you."

We all can't live in the "deserts of northern New Jersey" and the manifold oases like this around this country and indeed the whole world. There is a desert also in the heart of every city, and in the heart of every person.

But thank God for those who hear the tornado words of Saint Paul and are driven by the Spirit into our desert places, who lose themselves in silence and adoration. Thank God they offer hospitality and refuge to overstimulated, overwhelmed, overactive priestly minds who need from time to time to retreat and be renewed — to fast and pray, and soak in holy leisure and rest in the Lord and watch the deer disappear into the dark woods — before compline.

Dominican Priest, Prior, Pastor

Opening the Intellect

It is so hard to learn how to truly listen. I often find myself reading quickly to get to the end so that I can move on to something new. The Bethlehem desert experience created a sacred and safe space for me to experience something different. It created the environment for my intellect to relax, slow down and be open.

I remember being on retreat during the winter. I was seated at my desk looking out the large picture window. There was a slight covering of snow on the ground. The trees were bare except for a single leaf hanging on the tree before my window. I watched how the wind blew it back and forth. It hung in there; it refused to let go. I opened the Scriptures for the day and my eyes fell on the passage: "Let this mind be in you, which was also in Christ. He always had the very nature of God, but He did not think that by force He should try to become equal to God. Instead of His own free will He gave it all up, and took the nature of a servant" (Ph 2:5-7).

> An old man said: "Constant prayer quickly straightens out our thoughts."
>
> (DW, p. 32)

I read the passage a few times slowly and reflectively. As the word moved deeper within me, I realized that I was very much like that leaf. I did not want to let go. I did not want to become something other than what I was. My intellect has been opened long enough for a seed of wisdom to be planted.

I never did see the leaf fall from the tree. It was still hanging there when I left.

The *Lectio Divina* is a rich part of the Christian tradition. It presents the foundation for praying the Scriptures and spiritual reading. Simply put, it invites one to not only read a passage but to reflect on it, pray over it from the heart and then rest in the power of the Word to do what needs to be done. Practically, this is done by reading the same passage three times, once for reflecting, once for responding and once for resting in the Word.

Doing a *Lectio Divina* reading with the Scriptures for the next day's liturgy is a good practice. You also might like to apply the technique to reading other books. Set up a reading program for the coming year.

Diocesan Priest, Retreat Director, Lecturer

The Desert Experience and Our Emotional Life:
A Psychologist's Perspective

Why a retreat now, especially with such a busy life that includes managing an Alcohol Treatment facility with over 150 patients, an active family life with all the responsibilities that go hand in hand with that, and all the other distractions of modern life that afflict us all? But more than this, why a retreat of solitude, especially when I haven't been on a retreat since my high school days? How did this *call to the desert* come about? Since I can recall no initiation of the idea on my own, the fact that it not only just occurred to me *out of the blue* but also involved an almost uncanny magnetism, seemed to suggest that it emanated from a deeper place — from a Source greater than myself. It struck to my very existence. How would I explain to my wife, sons and co-workers that I would be taking off for a week to live in solitude? Such an alien notion in today's secular world does not get met with an immediate acceptance nor understanding. I concluded that this was a call by God to confront a very mysterious unknown.

A hunter in the desert saw Abba Antony enjoying himself with the brothers, and he was shocked. Wanting to show him that it was necessary sometimes to meet the needs of the brothers, the old man said to him, "Put an arrow in your bow and shoot it." So he did. And the old man said, "Shoot another," and he did so. Then the old man said, "Shoot yet again," and the hunter replied, "If I bend my bow so much, I will break it." Then the old man said to him, "It is the same with the work of God. If we stretch the brothers beyond measure, they will soon break. Sometimes, it is necessary to come down to meet their needs." (DRDF, p. 45)

God does not begin grand designs with a great deal of fanfare. He seems to choose humble beginnings to effect the call to transformation of lives. What was Bethlehem if not the consummate humble beginning for what is the single greatest transformative event of the ages? And so, I was called to the Hermitage of Bethlehem to begin what I believe was my own journey of transformation.

The Rule of Life of the Hermits of Bethlehem states that "we come to God as human beings with our emotions, fears, anxieties, irrationalities, angers, struggles, temptations and often sinful tendencies that need healing." In the field of psychological counseling, we use a variety of intrapersonal, as well as interpersonal technologies and strategies in an effort to help people cope more effectively with their lives, enhance their self efficacy and to achieve a greater harmony between themselves and the world in which they live daily. The field of addictions treatment, my area of specialization, has a history of tapping into the most fundamental sources of human healing, far more effectively than psychological theories have on their own been able to devise. This came with the advent of Alcoholics Anonymous in the late 1930's. The founders of AA understood right from the beginning that for people to achieve restored health, they had to undergo a basic transformation in their relationships with others, with self and with God. This was to be done by an admission of one's powerlessness and a recognition that only by turning one's life and will over to a power greater than one's self could recovery occur. In effect, this involved an act of *kenosis* — a dying to one's self, an emptying of all that is false in order to re-connect with one's true self, where an intimate relationship with God becomes possible.

The basic truths of AA and all successful psychological treatment recognize the spiritual dimension of our human nature, which is to say that we are created by God and intended by Him to share in His life. When, through sin, we rely more and more on the things of the world to sustain us, our emotions, intellect, even our will become tangled, chaotic and confused. Psychological healing can, however, take us just so far and often fails in that it does not recognize that men and women become most estranged from *themselves* when they are estranged from their Creator. We are inextricably linked to God; when we lose contact with Him as our Source, we necessarily become alienated from ourselves. This is so because we are created solely to participate in God's life. The restoration of our emotional health returns as our relationship with God is restored.

The desert experience allows us to participate in a *kenosis*, an emptying of all the emotionally compulsive ways that have become substitutes for the Real Presence of God in our lives. This Real Presence is mirrored for us in the uniquely intimate relationship that is shared between Jesus and His Father — a relationship to which we are likewise called. The desert experience gives us a unique opportunity to share in the Bread of Life — the Eucharistic Jesus — and regain our lost relationship with God. Like the manna in the desert that fed the Israelites' physical emptiness, the Bread of the Real Presence nourishes our spiritual and emotional emptiness. In the solitude of the desert, our emotional turmoil is reduced to the simple truth — that our life has one source and one alone which is our unique loving relationship with the God Who created us. We are destined to share in the same loving relationship that perfectly exists between God and His beloved Son, Jesus. This love is embodied in the Eucharist — the Bread that sustains our life in all its aspects — physically, spiritually, intellectually and emotionally. Having received the Bread of asceticism, we leave the desert to return to our everyday lives with a clearer vision of what truly feeds us emotionally — our life-giving relationship with God through His Son. In the end, for me, the desert experience has resulted in greater peace with myself — my emotions, my relationships, and my will — simply because, through Jesus, God and I have fallen in love again.

We are God's chosen people. We are called by Him to love and be loved, which is to say, to share in God's life. Many of us in our broken selves, from a psychological perspective, share in only one side of this equation to the detriment of the other. This distortion may lead us to emphasize loving others exclusively in a co-dependent or addictive fashion. In this way we love others as a substitute for loving ourselves — a love of which we feel most unworthy. An emphasis on the other side of the equation, i.e., looking *to be loved* to the exclusion of loving others, results in the narcissism that besets our age. The third way our loving becomes unbalanced is when God does not figure into the loving equation at all.

Our first task is to begin the process of restoring the foundation for life which is our relatedness to God. The desert experience allows this process to begin and to deepen. But from a psychological, as well as a spiritual, perspective this cannot occur without there necessarily occurring a closer examination of how well we love ourselves and others.

From a practical point of view, those of us who are in the healing professions, and especially those who are receiving psychological counseling, should make certain that healing involves attention to all three aspects of our life — our relationship with ourselves, others and most especially with God. Recovery from emotional woundedness can only take place fully when the spirit is healed, as well as the emotions and the body.

Husband, Father, Psychologist

Fasting

I first came to Bethlehem Hermitage with my Spiritual Director because I was having difficulty in learning to accept and understand one of the many gifts God has blessed me with. Just as some "demons" are only cast out through "prayer and fasting," I believe some of the problems and questions we face in life are only resolved and understood through "prayer and fasting," where we have the opportunity to come to the Lord, acknowledging our dependence on Him. I felt that I needed a time to just rest with Jesus in a place where I would be able to participate in Mass each day and be sustained with God's Word and the Sacrament of the Eucharist. I was fortunate to be able to spend a week at Bethlehem where just such an opportunity presented itself. With the Desert Father's blessing and permission, I was allowed to experience a total fast for most of the week, nourished by the Eucharist and feasting only on the Word of God. At Bethlehem, I found a place where the distractions we face in the world were removed and I was able to come into the Lord's presence with a heart centered on Him, recognizing that without the presence of Christ within us, we have nothing. I am still having difficulty accepting His gifts and understanding what His will is for me, but I know that no matter who we are, no matter how humble or simple our "station" is in this life, each one of us has a place in God's plan, each one of us is held in His hand, each one of us is loved and nourished and sustained with and in His love.

> We came from Palestine to Egypt and went to see one of the Fathers. He offered us hospitality and we said, "Why do you not keep the fast when visitors come to see you? In Palestine they keep it." He replied, "Fasting is always with me but I cannot always have you here. It is useful and necessary to fast but we choose whether we will fast or not. What God commands is perfect love. I receive Christ in you and so I must do everything possible to serve you with love. When I have sent you on your way, then I can continue my rule of fasting. The sons of the Bridegroom cannot fast while the Bridegroom is with them; when he is taken away from them, then they will fast."
>
> (DRDF, p. 44)

Why do I fast? Fasting helps me center myself on God. I think that the idea of fasting cannot be thought of outside the context of our worshipping. It's very humbling to realize that one of the first things Jesus addresses in the Gospels (Mt 6) has to do with the reasons for fasting. It's easy to take something we think of as good and try to use it to get God to do something we want. There seems to be so much emphasis on the blessings from fasting that it's tempting to think that with a little fast now and then we could have God practically eating out of our hands. But actually when we fast we should only be centering ourselves on God, opening our minds and hearts to His will. For it is in our *eating out of God's hands* that we will find freedom and peace and joy. Every other purpose is secondary.

Fasting should be entered into with prayer, initiated by God. If the sole purpose of my fasting is not a response to a call from Christ, done for the greater honor and glory of God, then I have failed in all I have attempted to do. Nothing can ever replace God as the center and source of fasting. For if I lose the object and purpose, I risk loving the blessing more than the Blesser, just as so many people love creation without ever catching sight of the Creator. I see Jesus' teaching on fasting in the Sermon on the Mount within the context of praying and giving, almost as if it is a given that praying and fasting and giving are all parts of Christian living.

Once the main reasons for our fasting are firmly planted in our hearts, we can explore other reasons and some of the blessings given to us in fasting. I think fasting, more than anything else, forces me to focus on the things of the world that control me. It seems that all of the controlling influences in my life surface during a fast and, as David tells us in Psalm 69:11, "fasting humbles the soul." Jealousy, anger, pride, fear — any of these things that bury themselves within us surface during a fast. For example, we may take a certain pride in the fact that we are *doing* something for God, and try to rationalize our accomplishments as being of our own doing. Then we come to the realization that it is not us, but the Spirit of God within us that is working. As for ourselves, we are giving in to the spirit of pride within us. We may be aggravated with someone or something, letting our aggravation take control in a burst of temper. At first, again we may try to rationalize the frustration and anger as a result of the hunger from our fasting. Then we realize that we are only frustrated and angry because we have lost sight of Christ within us and are giving in to the spirit of discord within us. Knowing that the power of Christ is within us and that healing is available is cause for worship and rejoicing in the Lord.

Fasting also helps me maintain some degree of balance in my life. In fasting I am able to deny myself something that is good and normal for the purpose of intensifying my relationship with our Lord. It is so easy to let unimportant *things* take precedence in our lives. It's incredible how easily we *need* things that are non-essential and how

81

easy it is to let these things enslave us. Eating in and of itself is good. I believe all of the normal functions of our life are good, but in fasting we are able to move the area of our concentration from the temporal things given to us in this life for our enjoyment to the kingdom of God and His glory; to the joy that is only found in resting in Jesus. It isn't always necessary to fast from food — we can just as easily fast from television, the media, the telephone, perhaps even people.

> *Abba Isidore said, "If you fast regularly, do not be inflated with pride; if you think highly of yourself because of it, then you had better eat meat. It is better for a man to eat meat than to be inflated with pride and glorify himself."* (DRDF, p. 40)

We are fed propaganda today that tries to convince us that if we don't have three meals a day with adequate snacks in between we will be on the verge of starvation. We are constantly told that if we fail to satisfy our every human appetite, we are in danger of missing out on things we are convinced we *deserve*. Our culture has thus reached a point where fasting as a discipline is almost obsolete. But I don't hear Jesus saying, "If you fast." I hear Him saying, "When you fast." Moses, Daniel, Esther, Elijah, Anna, Paul and Jesus Himself all fasted. And yet I don't hear Him saying this as if it were a Commandment. I hear Him teaching those who will fast how to fast and guiding their hearts toward union with Him.

As Paul tells us in 1 Corinthians 10, "Everything is lawful, but not everything is beneficial. . . not everything builds up. . . . eat anything. . . without raising questions on the grounds of conscience, for 'the earth and its fullness are the Lord's'" and most important "So whether you eat or drink, or whatever you do, do everything for the glory of God."

And we soon learn that it is not food that sustains us, but it is God that sustains us. "One does not live by bread alone, but by every word that comes forth from the mouth of God" (Mt 4:4). Fasting gives us the opportunity to feast on God's Word, just as Jesus was feasting when He said, "I have food to eat of which you do not know. . . My food is to do the will of the One Who sent Me" (Jn 4:32, 34).

I believe the feasting we are able to do on God's Word is also the reason Jesus tells us, "When you fast, anoint your head and wash your face, so that you may not appear to be fasting, except to your Father who sees what is hidden and will repay you. . . Is not life more than food and the body more than clothing?" (Mt 6:17-18, 25). We are told to be joyful when we fast, and rightly so, for we are feasting on the Word of God and just as the Israelites were sustained by the manna in the desert, we are sustained by the Word of God.

Laywoman, Comptroller

Solitude and Fasting

My first encounters with the desert experience of silence and solitude go back twenty years in my life. These moments on the spiritual journey have been an oasis of refreshment and strength. There have been times in my life that I have been lonely or isolated myself, but somehow the time of drawing apart in silence and solitude has been an experience of *being with* rather than one of aloneness. It has been for me an experience of *being with* the Lord.

I have been a priest for thirty years. I have had a wonderful life of many varied experiences of ministry and have met many good people. Over the years I have been a parish priest, a campus minister, worked with the charismatic movement, been the pastor of a parish, and currently am a chaplain at a large state prison.

As a prison chaplain, I do battle with the powers and principalities of the kingdom of darkness. I also witness the power of Jesus over the power of evil. I come to Bethlehem to be alone with Jesus and to pray for all the men I try to serve. I have a deep conviction that ministry built on prayer moves mountains. Over and over again I have seen it to be true.

Silence and solitude are not an end in themselves. They provide an environment in which we can be attentive to the quiet voice of the Spirit calling us to greater surrender to the Lord. To spend a day out of a busy life isn't easy. It takes planning ahead so that we give to the Lord the same time we would give to a friend. I can always find excuses for postponing the time with the Lord but I am fooling myself. In the ministry at the prison only the Lord can build the house. If the Lord doesn't go before me to touch the hearts of the men, nothing happens. When I pray and am listening to the Lord, the Spirit leads me to the right man at the right moment. I have had some beautiful experiences of grace as I have visited throughout the prison.

The spiritual bones of our lives get laid bare in the silence of the desert. A spiritual sight begins to develop; fasting especially helps to tune up the receptivity to the Lord and His Spirit. Self-denial with food is not easy for me; I love to eat. I can't always handle a growling stomach, but the practice grows if we begin in small ways. Fasting isn't meant to get in the way of our prayer.

I am trying to organize my life so that several times a month I come to Bethlehem. I need the spiritual power it gives me for my ministry at the prison and to keep at my own journey of conversion and surrender to Him.

Diocesan Priest, Prison Ministry

Love Isn't Love Until We Give It Away

Several years ago a good friend spoke of Bethlehem as a *special place, a place of wonder and surprise*! She issued the same challenge given years ago in Galilee, "Come and see!" (Jn 2:39).

Since then, Bethlehem has become not only a place of special gifts — but a place that has no boundaries; a silent voice echoing out and speaking of peace to aching hearts.

God of my Surprises! It was here that my new work came to birth — a new call, a new challenge, a new command for me — one to work in service to teenagers with AIDS. In the quiet of the woods, that voice would not be stilled — it just wouldn't go away!

God of my Insanity! "One of us has lost our mind," I whispered. In days of quiet unrest the voice kept growing — God of my Persistence! — and so the gentle hermit smiled and with a peaceful sigh, merely said, "Why not?"

And so I began "Rainbow House" — a sign of vision and hope, the sign of God taking me where I did not plan to go!

In reflecting upon the message of Bethlehem, it seems to me that it is so wonderful to touch those special moments of union as we wander wooded hills, or bow in wonder at the silence of the Eucharistic Presence.

Yet the real message of Bethlehem began in the moments following His Birth in which Mary began at once to give Him away — to smelly shepherds, terrifying strange kings, doubting townsfolk, angry crowds, and finally cruel soldiers. Today, our Bethlehem begins as we give Him to our families, to the poor, the unwashed, the unchurched, the unlovely who wander among us. We are asked to see Him in the depressed and demanding neighbor, the AIDS baby, the pregnant teen, those most likely to slip through the cracks of society. In the stillness of Bethlehem carried into our world we hear the muted cry, begging us to give each day; it is there that *love* reaches out in *us*, from Bethlehem's straw.

Sister of Charity of St. Elizabeth, Convent Station, New Jersey

Expanded Awareness

God has given me a great opportunity in being alone with Him at Bethlehem. Bethlehem has brought desert spirituality into my life in a vivid and colorful way. Through denial, silence and solitude, I am enriched with and can enjoy God's good gifts in me, God's words and God's presence in others. When I retreat from the world and surrender myself to be alone with God, I find a profound and penetrating awareness. There is an atmosphere of awe, in which centering prayer is richly enhanced by the remote surroundings of God's creation.

Desert spirituality is a witness of surrender that binds God's love to my desire of service. Through my Bethlehem retreats, God has refreshed and recreated me, so that I may minister His love in my family and community. My retreats at Bethlehem always bring me an enlivened spirit. I am aware of an intimacy with God my Creator. I am refreshed through my aloneness with God. I am recreated and anticipate reaching out to my family and community in love.

Through my desert spirituality, God has led me into my church as a Lector and my community as a Hospice volunteer. Speaking God's words and sharing in the sorrows and the pain of suffering people, has brought to me a beautiful understanding of God's love and compassion. There is an expanded awareness of a need for empathy and compassion within my heart that would not have been possible without contemplative prayer which I have experienced as refreshment, through my retreats at Bethlehem.

Bethlehem has become such a beautiful part of my daily life, I have set up a *Bethlehem prayer corner* in a prominent area of my home. A Nativity set is at the center and is a reminder of the gift of Jesus, of the gift of His Word, and of His Presence in the Eucharist.

I awake at five a.m. for my daily prayers. This is a pleasant time of the day for me, with its stillness and peace. I read the psalms and Scripture for thirty minutes and then I relax and absorb the presence of God in centering prayer and we dwell in each other. This is a time I have set apart to focus on and to converse with my Creator. I rejoice in God my Savior.

Husband, Father

The Bread of Hospitality

True to the sacred spot that inspired its name and its mission, Bethlehem is a place where people come and go. They come to see Jesus and they find Him with Mary, His mother, and St. Joseph. And they go, like the shepherds and the kings, rejoicing at what they saw and heard, eager to spread abroad the good news — news that is now, for them, not only hear-say or prophecy, but a reality in their lives.

Even before the construction of hermitages or a central house or a chapel on the grounds of Bethlehem in Chester, New Jersey, the virtue of hospitality was practiced there. During the time when Father Romano resided temporarily at Mr. Frank Van Alen's farmhouse, he still welcomed visitors to view the property and to pray with him for the success of his endeavor.

I can recall the day I phoned Father Romano and heard him announce for the first time: "Bethlehem Center!" There was a tone of joyful conviction in Father's voice that implied: "This is it! We're on the way!" At last his dream was beginning to take shape. And that voice epitomized the tone of welcome, the warm reception that greeted whoever came to Bethlehem.

> A brother came and stayed with a certain solitary and when he was leaving he said, "Forgive me, Father, for I have broken in upon your rule." But the hermit replied, saying, "My Rule is to receive you with hospitality and let you go in peace." (WD, p. 51, #75)

When Bethlehem Hermitage was Bethlehem Center — in the early days of its existence — hospitality meant being absorbed into whatever was in progress at the time. Was the community at prayer? You were handed a prayer book and the page was pointed out to you. Were they at a meal? You were invited to the table to partake of whatever was being served (a round table is conducive to allowing for one more). If it was recreation time, you found yourself quickly drawn into the circle of conversation and laughter as if you always belonged there. Spiritual subjects were introduced and discussed easily and naturally. And, yes, you might find yourself pouring coffee, clearing the table, or washing dishes. Even such chores as these are enjoyable when the company is agreeable. It is not difficult to rise above the material and mundane when religion is viewed and experienced as a well-balanced, beautiful, cheerful way of life. It was so at the start and is still so at Bethlehem in Chester, New Jersey.

Now that the lifestyle of the community has been refined and formalized, the approach is different, but the same warm spirit of welcome is felt everywhere. The hermits live a life of constant prayer and close union with Jesus in the Eucharist. They overflow with joy and kindness as they serve silently the needs of retreatants and of each other. During Holy Mass the same welcoming is expressed — now to the whole Church in the embrace of the Eucharistic Sacrifice and in the breaking of bread.

And because the *bread of hospitality* offered at Bethlehem is as wholesome and substantial as home-made bread — satisfying and nourishing — the effects remain long after one has left the house. There is a yearning for more of the same and an inclination to make one's own environment as much like Bethlehem as it can be.

This can be accomplished by being ever more conscious of the Divine Presence within our own souls and in the souls of all those we meet. We desire to make this prayer our own:

"O Most Holy Trinity Who dwells by grace in my soul, grant that all those who come into contact with me this day may feel the power of Your Presence and be drawn to love You."

For we must learn how to welcome God into our own lives before we are able to show hospitality to His people.

Sister of Charity of St. Elizabeth
Convent Station, New Jersey

88

To Be a "House of Bread"

Romans 8:9 says, "If anyone does not have the Spirit of Christ, he is not His." Jesus described Himself as the Bread of Life (Jn 6:35): "He who eats this Bread will live forever." We partake of Jesus as the Bread of Life by our faith in Him, repenting of our sins and acknowledging Him as our Savior and Lord. It is then that the Spirit of Jesus — the Holy Spirit — takes up residence in us and *we* become little Bethlehems, Houses of Bread.

> *Abba Poemen said, "There is no greater love than that a man lays down his life for his neighbor. When you hear someone complaining and you struggle with yourself and do not answer him back with complaints; when you are hurt and bear it patiently, not looking for revenge; then you are laying down your life for your neighbor."* (DRDF, p. 50)

My experience at Bethlehem Hermitage has been a renewal that has given me an ever greater awareness of the Bread of Life within me so that I have more of Jesus to share with others when I leave.

I believe that those called to share the charism (ministry or service) of Bethlehem Hermitage will already be a House of Bread — the Living Bread. Jesus will already be living within them through the Holy Spirit. They will hear the call to come to Bethlehem Hermitage not only because they hunger for deeper fellowship with Jesus, but because they hunger to offer more of Jesus to those who come seeking Him. They will know the truth of our Lord's words, "It is more blessed to give than to receive."

Husband, Father, Episcopalian Minister

Renewed in the Hospitality of God

The Lord has been good to me as a priest for the last fifteen years and has especially blessed me with a month's stay at Bethlehem Hermitage. I have made retreats before but never with the same 24-hour prayerful atmosphere. The silence and solitude made me available to the Lord as I never was before. In silence the Scripture really penetrated my heart like the rain in the desert and gradually led to penitence and a deeper heartfelt understanding of His mercy.

In solitude before the Blessed Sacrament, I became more honest and less filled with other concerns so that all the words of God and the events of daily life naturally spoke to my heart of God's love for me.

This silent and solitary desert experience was offered by the Hermits of Bethlehem, a warm, loving and human Laura of Hermits who encouraged me by their silent hospitality to relax and be renewed in the hospitality of God.

The spirit of Bethlehem will always be alive in me as I return to Japan. There, many people are looking for more in life — and I hope to share the fruits of Bethlehem with them so that they can *taste and see how good the Lord is.*

I thank the Bethlehem Desert Father for his warm welcome and kindness to me, the kind Hermits of Bethlehem and the good benefactors of Bethlehem Hermitage who made this all possible.

I remember all of you in my prayers with gratitude in the Sacred Hearts of Jesus and Mary.

Missionary Priest of the Sacred Hearts of Jesus and Mary,
Native of Japan

Desert Day*

Bethlehem Hermitage has been a place and an opportunity to come home to God. The pine tree haven, the solitude, and the Word provide

---

* The term "Desert Day" has been changed to "Day of Reclusion" to reflect the deeper solitude we experience on that day of the week.

a welcome time to spend with God. It is a place where God speaks and you listen.

Bethlehem Hermitage Desert Days offer another means of encounter with God through fasting, silence and the Word. The Desert Days taught me the value of allowing even my body, mind and spirit to hunger for God.

As a parish priest, and now a pastor, I have struggled with how to introduce what I have experienced of Desert Day with others. Three years ago, our parish staff brainstormed ways to bring the Desert Day experience to the parish. It is certainly an abbreviated approach to what the Bethlehem Hermitage offers but nonetheless graced for us at this time.

At the end of our Wednesday Eucharistic Liturgy, we explain briefly the intent of the Desert Day experience whether or not you work inside or outside the home. We ask people to adjust their normal activities of the day: perhaps fast from the radio, TV, talking unnecessarily, fast from food if possible, and be attentive to the whisperings of God throughout the day — in prayer, meditation, or the Word. We bless bread using the same formula as at Bethlehem. After the final blessing and dismissal we invite people to a video presentation and brief discussion and then departure. We find that the video presentation assists people in their spiritual development. This year we have included once-a-month adoration of the Blessed Sacrament from 10:00 a.m. to noon on our Desert Day. We believe God works through nature and is continuing to lead us and direct us at a pace we can handle with Him.

I owe my understanding and development of my spiritual hunger to Bethlehem where I learned the way of contemplative prayer. Centering Prayer has been a prayer form that is compatible with my personality. It has brought me to many wonderful moments with God. In addition, the Hermits of Bethlehem have led me to the value of a spiritual life through the means of Desert Days. I am proud to be able to share this as best I can with the people here on the journey. And I realize that God will continue to reveal to us how we can grow with our Desert Day.

It is humbling to know that in a small but significant way we share this Day with the Hermits of Bethlehem. May God be praised for the blessings we share.

This is the way we invite our parishioners to participate in Desert Day:

"Then the Spirit led Jesus into the desert. . ." (Mt 4:1).

In both the Old Testament tradition and the New Testament, the desert is the place of encounter with the Lord. In the desert experience, the will of God is more clearly grasped and commitment is strengthened to do what God desires.

It is in the "desert" that God invites a person to enter into a deeper relationship with Him. We come before God in trust and confidence and experience God's welcome, love, forgiveness and peace. We also come in contact with God's desire to share those very things with others through the way we live our own lives.

Even today we can tap the wisdom of spending time with the Lord through a "desert experience." Some of the pieces of a desert experience that are suggested by our tradition are solitude or quiet, prayer, and fasting. The way we approach these different pieces may be as unique as the circumstances of our lives.

We invite you to enter into our "Desert Day" on Wednesday in the ways that you discover are best for you. Though you might not be able to spend the time in solitude, you might want to bring to the day a *spirit of quiet*, a way of moving through the day more aware of God's presence.

In prayer, we can find ways to discover, recognize, and respond to the God Who is always seeking us. You might want to spend some time with the Scriptures or pray from your heart to God. Our parish intention is that we discover and follow the will of God for us as the parish community of _____ Parish.

Fasting is a practice which reminds us that as hungry people we are very much in need of God and of one another. Fasting sometimes means not eating certain things. Sometimes it means eating very little or not at all for a period of time. You might want to choose some kind of fast that you are able to do on Wednesday. We can fast not only from food, but also from whatever dulls our sense of God — from negative thoughts, from angry words, from TV, from living in the fast lane.

On *Wednesdays*, our *Desert Days*, blessed bread is distributed after the _____ a.m. Mass to strengthen us in our fast of choice. We will also have a short video after Mass to "seed" our minds and hearts with some topic that relates to our faith-life.

Everyone is welcome to join us for the video and reflection.

All are invited to participate in some way in this Desert Experience.

Pastor, Archdiocese of Newark

Celibacy and Solitude

I have spent many days at Bethlehem, moments set apart from my ordinary and hectic schedule at a large university. As a diocesan priest, I live my life in service to God's people. That is why I was ordained. Yet, more fundamentally, I know that I am their servant for the sake of Jesus. It was this Jesus Who first touched my heart with that amazing grace to see Him, to believe in Him; to spend my life for His Name. Nurturing and developing that relationship with the living Lord is one of the more important calls I have. And, perhaps better put, it is one of the most important things I am. I go to Bethlehem and enter into solitude to find anew that voice which first called me and which continues to beckon my heart in new and ever-different ways.

As a man who has freely accepted the Lord's call — and gift — to be single for His sake and for the sake of His Gospel, I rely on His words that those who have forgone wife and children, parents and property in this life will have a hundredfold now and in the world to come eternal life. I know that this hundredfold is realized in relationship to the Lord. *He* is that treasure, *His word* is that pearl of great price, *His life and grace* are that hundredfold. But I will never recognize that gift if I do not take the grist of my daily living and read it with the eyes of faith. It is in the days and the hours that Bethlehem provides that I have the chance to hear, to see and to know, in ways that I usually do not experience, the love and the grace of this living God in Jesus Christ.

The solitude of Bethlehem helps me to *see*, in a God-graced way. The desert experience helps me to see celibacy, my gift of self to the Lord, as a condition for my experience of the risen Jesus.

Bethlehem and the solitude of quiet days help to remove the *scales* which block my sight of the things that are most real, most important in me and around me, the things that are of the Kingdom of the Father.

Solitude gives me the time of grace to see who I am before the Lord. The distractions which are part of ordinary living in ministry are minimal in Bethlehem. All those truths which tend to get drowned out in routines are suddenly recognized again — and treasured anew; sun and sky; dawn and dusk; the sounds of creation and the beat of the earth. But more than the voice of the Lord's created work is heard. The longings and affections of my heart are revealed. The living Word speaks in silence, the Whisper-Who-Is-Love makes Himself heard by my heart. This is not some kind of lofty mysticism, simply the voice of a good and caring Father, uninterrupted by the cacophony of the world.

The days that are spent at Bethlehem and in other retreats make all the difference in the ways I live my celibate life, with its rushing and its demands, in a spirit of praise, gratitude and joy.

Celibacy, if it is anything, is life lived as fully as possible for the Lord, for His Word and for His Kingdom.

To be celibate is to live in awareness that one has been called and chosen by the Lord to be *for Him*, and for Him alone.

This requires generous periods of time given to prayer and to a contemplative experience of the Lord's word and presence.

Regular retreats, days of prayer and times of solitude are important ingredients in establishing and maintaining that contact with the Lord. For me, concretely, this means one day each month which I try to spend, in silence, away from the calls of normal ministry. More practically, and specifically, the Lord wants some time of solitude each day. This is the desert experience on a daily basis.

Diocesan Priest, Professor

His All-Powerful Love and Wisdom

Celibate hermits believe so strongly in the saving power of the love of Jesus that they resolutely answer His call to stand before the throne of the Lamb worshipping Him with their whole being, believing firmly that His all-powerful love and wisdom flow from Jesus through them to those actively building His Kingdom in the world. This is a call that one hears in the very depths of one's spirit. It is answered by those who have truly experienced the mystery of their resurrected Lord. It is a sacrificial answer, for one seldom sees results.

Two monks, on their way to the monastery, found an exceedingly beautiful woman at the riverbank. Like them, she wished to cross the river, but the water was too high. So one of the monks lifted her onto his back and carried her across.

His fellow monk was thoroughly scandalized. For two hours he berated him on his negligence in keeping the rule: Had he forgotten he was a monk? How did he dare touch a woman? And worse, carry her across the river? What would people say? Had he not brought their holy religion into disrepute? And so on.

The offending monk listened patiently to the never-ending sermon. Finally he broke in with, "Brother, I dropped that woman at the river. Are you still carrying her?"

(SB, p. 108)

Among the Hermits of Bethlehem, I have witnessed the answer to this call. These hermits portray the power of God, not as the world depicts power but in the strength of silent, gentle, loving lives lived in service to those who come to seek the Lord. Their service stretches out in a loving, sacrificial, mysterious way to those who live amidst the turmoil of the world.

I have spent a week each year for the past ten years living among these hermits. Each year I acquire a deeper meaning of:

— my own creaturehood as I experience the presence of my Creator each day at a Liturgy filled with the mystery of our gentle, silent, powerful Lord in Word and Sacrament.

— the stillness of the surrounding atmosphere, for I have come to realize the truth of the words of the Psalmist: "Be still and know that I am God" (Ps 46:10).

— service as I see in the resident hermits a selflessness and a gentle care for others that flow from hearts filled to overflowing with the charity of Christ.

Yes, I have grown deeper as a result of my contact with the hermits of Bethlehem and in the depths of my own being I find the compassion, the love and the deep worship of Jesus growing within me. I will ever be grateful to them for the manner in which they bear witness to their vowed life, especially the vow of celibacy.

Sister of Charity of New York

Celibate Love — Chastity

St. Paul says: "I should like you to be free of all worries. The unmarried person is busy with the Lord's affairs, concerned with pleasing the Lord. . . The virgin — indeed — is concerned with things of the Lord, in pursuit of holiness in body and spirit" (1 Cor 7:32-34).

For me Bethlehem represents a reminder, a concrete, beautiful reminder that the Lord is my first priority. As a single person committed to God, I need the time and space to develop and foster my relationship with God. Being at Bethlehem allows me to slow down and realize that God is already here in my heart, loving me.

The remembrance of God creates a desire to love Him and be with Him, and hollows out a space where our relationship grows and deepens. Bethlehem reminds me that I need this time and space, that

I need to be present to God, allowing Him to love me so I can love Him in return.

The natural setting of Bethlehem Hermitage draws me to God: the deer frolicking in the field and wooded areas; the little chipmunks scampering into the woodpile; the clean, fresh smell of pine — these call me to God, to adore Him, to revel in His presence, to appreciate Him, to enter into a deeper dimension of gratefulness and presence to Him, to love Him. I draw closer to God and surrender myself to be loved by Him and to love Him in return.

> One of the Fathers said, "No one can see his face reflected in muddy water; and the soul cannot pray to God with contemplation unless first cleansed of harmful thoughts." (WA, p. 143, #13)

We are called by God to love Him, our neighbor and ourselves. One way to do this is to be aware of His presence. The practice of the awareness of His presence can be cultivated by often returning to the Bethlehem of the heart.

This can be fostered by recollecting ourselves when we notice the sky, watch the leaves sway in the breeze, or pause to find the created beauty around us while stopped at a traffic light. These can be times for remembering God, being grateful to Him and loving Him.

Laywoman

A Poverty of Spirit Experience

As a Franciscan, I am committed on a daily basis to be actively engaged in the lives of many people. Such availability to others calls for a lot of detachment from self.

The vow of poverty, which is a complete dependence on the All-

Providing God, comes into work in that it creates the free time and space to be there and give of *self* to others.

My retreat experiences at the Bethlehem Hermitage with its solitude and challenging Desert Day have been great opportunities to take inventory on how well or poorly I am embracing *Lady Poverty*, that is, trusting and depending completely on God.

My initial yearning within the simplicity of the hermitage for TV, the boom box with rap music, soda, ice cream, and just someone to talk to are powerful reminders that I have a long way to go in living out poverty in my own life!

The quiet peacefulness, prayerfulness, and intimacy of the Bethlehem Desert Experience help to quiet me down to experience the immense love God has for me, and also to better hear where God is calling me to be available to others.

The healing and life-enriching experience of Bethlehem reawakens within me the importance of taking time daily to quiet down and get in touch with our God Who loves and cares for us deeply, but also to be detached enough, that is, free and available enough to awaken this same God in the lives of our sisters and brothers in our everyday lives.

A practical test to see how well one is living in poverty — that is, free enough to hear our God Who speaks daily to our hearts as well as to be free enough to be available to others — would be to carve in some *quiet time* during our day, be it at home, driving, school, or at work. We can take a shorter lunch hour, shut off the TV, or turn off the radio, and use this *quiet time* to hear our God speaking through the *chatter* of our lives.

Franciscan Priest

Freedom and Joy Through Poverty

Coming to the Bethlehem Hermitage for a retreat, one can only be awed and thankful for all that God is. In the quiet we become conscious that all we have, and all we are, have been given us as gifts by our Father. We become aware of God's call to us to follow His way — and our response in faith can only be to embrace His challenge and walk beside Him, for only then are we able to grow in holiness. During a stay at Bethlehem it becomes clear that only in removing from our lives those things which would sidetrack us or hinder our attempt to follow the Gospel, and only in using our gifts for their intended purpose, can we responsibly respond to our Father's call. The time given me at Bethlehem was one where I found the freedom to turn all of my attention to the Lord, to put myself completely at His disposal. It was a time when it was easy to sense God's presence in every gift, in every moment. St. Bonaventure said that "Experience proves beyond a doubt that it is impossible for a man to serve God perfectly unless he endeavors to divorce himself completely from the world. Our steps, disengaged from any worldly pursuit, are made free to follow the Redeemer: for as the Apostle says, 'No one serving as God's soldier entangles himself in worldly affairs.'" I'd like to share some of what I discovered at Bethlehem of the joy and peace and freedom found in poverty.

> Someone asked Amma Syncletica of blessed memory, "Is absolute poverty perfect goodness?" She replied, "It is a great good for those capable of it; even those who are not capable of it find rest for their souls in it though it causes them anxiety. As tough cloth is laundered pure white by being stretched and trampled underfoot, so a tough soul is stretched by freely accepting poverty."
>
> (DRDF, p. 34)

"He began to teach them saying, 'Blessed are the poor in spirit, for theirs is the kingdom of heaven...'" (Mt 5:3). Being open to Christ and the mystery of creation begins our prayer. By losing ourselves in the smells and sensations and sounds of the world, by searching beneath the surface of the people and creatures around us, we begin to hear God speak to us through all of creation. I think we learn a lot just by watching how God takes care of His creation.

Blow on the puffball of a dandelion and watch the little parachutes drift off on the lightest of breezes, some landing on fertile ground, some in rocky places. The thistle and the milkweed both have defenses to protect their nectar from the ants that would pillage it if they could. If you watch the ants as they crawl up the stem you will see that the tiniest of scratches from their feet make the milk come out and stick to their feet. As they try to wipe it off they only make the situation worse. . . and the nectar is saved for the Monarch butterfly — the milkweed's perfect pollinator. The thistle's downward bristles serve the same purpose, but as an added defence it has a band of sticky gum that acts like flypaper for any ant "fortunate" enough to get past the bristles. The thistle's nectar is saved for a beautiful butterfly called the Painted Lady who will pollinate the flower and insure its future.

When we look deeper into the things God has created, we see more than the beauty of the flowers and the idle fluttering of the butterflies. We see living individuals whose very existence depends upon God. We develop a finer appreciation for the wonderfully conceived universe God has created for us to live in. We lose our anxieties as we become more aware of His caring hands upon us — He will never abandon us for "He who began a good work among you will bring it to completion by the day of Jesus Christ" (Ph 1:6). I think it's especially important to know this when we are facing a struggle or when something we hope for is replaced by despair and things don't seem to be going as we feel they should. We must have faith that what we ask is not always what His will is for us. As we learn to surrender to His will, we can trust Him to do what is best for us every time. When we look to nature and see all the wonderful work God has done in making all things work together, it's easy to see how the writer of Proverbs said, "Trust in the Lord with all your heart, and lean not on your own understanding; in all your ways acknowledge Him and He shall direct your paths" (Pr 3:5-6). We begin to realize that truly as we "seek the Kingdom of God. . . it is our Father's pleasure to give us the Kingdom" (Lk 12:31-32).

We can only praise our Father as our voices join the chorus of creation in praise to His glory; we can only pray that He will make us more sensitive to all of life and help us open our eyes to the world around us to see the possibilities of service and salvation through prayer and work that are always there. We can only pray He will make us more sensitive to the workings of the Spirit within us that our hearts might be filled with the love of Christ for all people and that we might share this love with everyone. And in our poverty we can only pray that we will remain humble, aware that every accomplishment for God is His work in us and in the Church we serve.

Laywoman, Secular Franciscan

What Is Really True Obedience?
or God Is Not Finished With Me Yet!

On the fourth day of my desert retreat, I sat in the chapel silently repeating the simple phrase, "Yes, Lord." I had no particular problem in mind. I had no conscious area of focus; just simply, "Yes, Lord. Yes, Lord. Yes, Lord. . . ."

During my evening meal, I wondered what had prompted the prayer. I didn't think of myself as disobedient. I didn't recall deliberate disobedience to God's commandments. Yet, there was a tension within me as I thought about the word *obedience*. In bed, I found myself again repeating "Yes, Lord. Yes, Lord. . ." more to ease the tension than anything else.

In the morning, I thought about who I am. I'm a take-charge kind of person in a world that thrives on competition and prizes; the *I did it my way* mentality. Perhaps I don't have a problem with flagrant disobedience, but how many times do I respond to those in authority with obedience to the letter, but not the spirit? How many times do I obey with a scowl or a mean disposition or even open grumbling? How many times do I *do it my way* and count myself virtuous because my way is obviously better than the way those in authority directed? As I thought about *obedience* as meaning *total obedience*, I had to confess that I obey in an approximate fashion, but I am not *submissive*.

I began to see that my relationship with the Lord is not too dissimilar. Being a good Catholic Christian is not the same thing as being totally submissive to God's will and His commandments.

Now the prayer, "Yes, Lord. Yes, Lord. Yes, Lord. . ." is my daily prayer. I don't know if I've achieved any greater obedience in these past months, but then, God is not finished with me yet.

We rarely think of obedience as being a virtue ranking near the top of God's list. We need to pray for obedience, but we should not expect that one day obedience will suddenly overcome us. We must look for daily opportunities to consciously and submissively obey; the boss, the traffic officer, the librarian, our pastor, our spouse, our parents. How about visiting the sick, not because we enjoy it, but because the Lord told us to? How about praying the rosary daily, not because it is our favorite form of prayer, but because the Mother of God asked us to?

Husband, Father, Executive

The Challenge of Listening

In the Rule of the Hermits of Bethlehem we encounter a beautiful explanation of the vow of obedience for the hermits. At the very same time, it is the call of all Christians, even those in the marketplace, even those who have other vocations than that of religious life, to live with an obedient heart. Obedience and the vow of obedience have fallen on hard times. People are concerned about and even afraid of obedience. Too often people have lived under tyrannical rule, being mistreated or treated as one less than human. Here, I am speaking about healthy, loving obedience. The obedient One is Jesus. Jesus listened most attentively to the call of the Father and was faithful to that call even unto death on a cross.

First of all, we know that the English word "obedience" comes from the Latin root "audire" which means "to listen." As I reflect on the vow of obedience in my life, I know that first I need to listen because I am a disciple. I need to listen to the voice of God in the depths of my being as well as in the church. If one does not listen, then one does not know what to do. The first vocation of all contemplatives, those who are hermits or in monastic enclosures and those of us in the marketplace, is to listen with the ears of the heart. Holy listening draws us even closer to God into a deeper relationship of heart speaking to heart.

> *Abba Mios of Belos said, "Obedience responds to obedience. When someone obeys God, then God obeys his request."* (DRDF, p. 28)

To live this vow of obedience for me as a diocesan priest who is the pastor of an inner city parish in Brooklyn, is for me to listen. I listen most attentively to my people where I, day in and day out, discover God. I listen so as to discover what I am to do since I have been entrusted with a ministry of service. I need to return each day to the quiet hermitage not made of stone and wood but of flesh. If I do not listen to God in quiet, I will not hear God in the people that God has entrusted to me.

I need to be obedient to my bishop since I am intimately connected with the ordinary of my diocese. Each diocesan priest looks to his bishop, listening to discover what to do so as to better serve God's people. The authority of my bishop and all bishops comes from the intimate connection each bishop has with God in the role of pastor. Holy listening is necessary so as to discern God's Spirit and to live most effectively the ministry of service.

Our bishop was looking for a priest to pastor the parish of St. Ann-St. George, a parish known for its poverty in an area where people have been hurt, forgotten and crushed down. Crime, violence and addiction plague our streets. The bishop wanted this place to become a Center of Evangelization. I heard the need; I volunteered to come, and I have set out to accomplish this. Holy listening implies that I give myself to the task because it is what God asks through the lips of my bishop.

Abba Hyperichius said, "The true service of a monk is obedience and if he has this, whatever he asks will be given him and he will stand with confidence before the Crucified. For that was how the Lord went to His Cross, being made obedient even unto death."

(DRDF, p. 80)

Holy listening in the daily routine of our lives is not possible unless we each day faithfully step apart and listen in silence. If we never take time to be quiet hermits each day, we will not know what it is God is saying. Our days, busy as they are, can have a hermit time as its hub, maybe ten minutes or an hour, but each day it is necessary to have some holy listening.

Periodically it is also necessary for us to go to the desert. Some of us have the privilege and opportunity to spend a week in the hermitage; for others, a day or two is what we can spend in whatever lifestyle we live. Periodic breaks with our business to simply listen is necessary and required if we are going to be holy listeners, with an obedient heart.

Diocesan Priest, Brooklyn

Obedience and Solitude

The very word "obedience" has a tendency to make me wince. It conjures up thoughts of "toeing the line" or "blind submission." If understood properly, however, obedience can be very fulfilling. The Bethlehem experience, for example, has given me a deeper appreciation of obedience. As a priest, in the silence of Bethlehem, I can say "Yes" to the Lord speaking through His legitimate representatives. I can say "Yes" without anger, bitterness or resentment. I want to be open to legitimate requests made of me. "My food is to do the will of the One Who sent Me, and to complete His work" (Jn 4:34). My obedience contributes to fulfilling my ministry as a priest. This brings joy.

When obedience does not come easy, I must look to the Lord. Bethlehem provides an atmosphere where I can humbly call upon the Spirit for enlightenment and guidance. In the solitude, I try to discern God's will. This process may seem monumental — it may take much time and effort. Yet, it is necessary because much is at stake. The danger is to make a mistake which later would be regretted. I do not want to selfishly obey my own will, but the will of God.

It is important to wait on the Lord and then obey. Perhaps John Henry Cardinal Newman (1801-1890) explained it best when he wrote:

> It was a lesson continually set before the Israelites, that they were never to presume to act of themselves, but to wait till God wrought for them, to look on reverently, and follow His guidance. God was their All-Wise King; it was their duty to have no will of their own, distinct from His will, to form no plan of their own, to attempt no work of their own. "Be still and know that I am God." Move not, speak not — look to the pillar of the cloud, see how *it* moves — then follow. Such was the command.
>
> *Parochial and Plain Sermons,* Ignatius Press, p. 492.

I believe that Bethlehem provides a spiritual oasis to "look on reverently and then follow His guidance."

It would be great if the Bethlehem Hermitage were located within walking distance of our houses — instant solitude and quiet. In reality, however, we must seek the Bethlehem experience wherever we may find ourselves. It may be a local park or, for the busy commuter, the confines of the car, without radio or cassette player on. We need to obey God's will. It will bring us fulfillment. In order to live meaningful lives, we are called into our "private desert" to wait upon the Lord. Like the Israelites of old, we, too, must "look on reverently, and follow His guidance."

Diocesan Priest, Diocese of Pittsburgh

The Bethlehem Hermits and the Church

For twelve years I have been a frequent visitor of this Hermitage, where I regularly return for spiritual direction and confession, for days of recollection, and for retreats; one was for thirty days. Each visit is a unique experience. I always feel myself to be an intimate part of the Church. As I leave to return to my apostolic work, I am closer to the evangelizing mission of the Church and I make efforts to help others appreciate the Mystical Body of Christ.

Here in this northern section of New Jersey, amid the quiet beauty and the whispering winds of the pines, I experience the presence of the Holy Spirit, as I read the welcoming words of the prophet Hosea: "I will espouse you (in faith) and lead you into the desert and there I will speak to your heart" (Ho 2:14).

It is here that I experience in a deeper way the richness of the Church and its treasures in the impressive liturgies, in the devout recital of the Divine Office, in moments of Adoration before the Blessed Sacrament, in the selected readings from Scripture and the Fathers of the Church. This spiritual oasis in Chester, New Jersey, is as much a part of the Universal Church as any Cathedral in our modern cities. The Spirit of God is present: "The Spirit of the Lord fills the whole world. It holds all things together" (Ws 1:7).

Away from the noise of the city, in the quiet of this country chapel, the weary traveller finds here peace and comfort: "Come to Me all you who are weary and tired, and I will give you rest" (Mt 11:28).

This spiritual oasis of Bethlehem Hermitage is for me a place of rest, prayer and listening to the Spirit.

The Hermits of Bethlehem in the Heart of Jesus are called by their consecrated life to be *Church* for the retreatants who come to rediscover the *amazing grace* that is *Church*. In this rustic chapel, in the stillness of adoration, the weary soul finds strength and comfort, the spiritually hungry and thirsty find food and drink for the long journey.

> *Abba Poemen related that Abba John said that the saints are like a group of trees, each bearing different fruit, but watered from the same source. The practices of one saint differ from those of another, but it is the same Spirit that works in all of them.* (DRDF, p. 68)

Like all gifts of the Spirit, the proper charism of Bethlehem Hermitage is for the building of the Body of Christ, the Church. This charism, embodied in the Rules, leads one to a deeper awareness of the Universal Church. The very life of the hermits is a genuine witness to Christ's love for His Spouse. Pope Paul VI said it so well when he spoke to a group of contemplatives: "You are by no means on the fringe of the Church, but you are in the very center of the Church, close to the Heart of God."

As Christians we are often invited to make acts of gratitude for the gift of Baptism. This sacrament marks us as members of the Faith Community and gives us a right to the prayers of the sacramental life of the Church. The more we realize this truth, the deeper will be our reverence for the House of God. How sad it is to see the sacredness of our churches lost to this generation! From the Hermitage we can bring to our own parish churches this gift of the sacred.

Salesian Priest of St. John Bosco

Bethlehem Prayer

Jesus, gentle and humble of Heart, You are the Bread of Life; help me to live my life hidden in Your Eucharistic Heart in the Presence of our Father united in the love and power of Your Holy Spirit.

Give me a listening heart, a heart to love You for Your own Sake, to love You in myself, and to love You in my brothers and sisters as You have loved.

Consume me in the fire of Your Love.

Mary, Mother of the Incarnate Word and my Mother, you are the first "house of bread."

Help me to live in perfect love by being:
the bread of Humility and Abandonment to the
Father's Will;
the bread of Purity of Heart;
the bread of Word and Eucharist;
the bread of Simplicity, Poverty and Littleness;
the bread of Silence and Solitude;
the bread of Prayer and Contemplation;
the bread of Reconciliation and Peace;
the bread of Interior and Joyful Suffering;
the bread of Charity and Hospitality, broken and
offered with Jesus to the Merciful Father and shared
for the salvation of the world.

Holy Mary, Lady of Bethlehem, Queen of the Desert, guide me in the journey of the Spirit that, together with you, I may participate in the wedding feast of the Risen Lamb until at last I may sing an eternal Magnificat of Love and Praise face to Face before our All-Holy Triune God. Amen.

Eugene L. Romano, HBHJ
Desert Father

Hermits of Bethlehem in the Heart of Jesus

Brief History and Origins

Begun as a rough, undefined idea honoring peace centered in Jesus, Source of Bread and Life, Bethlehem Hermitage in Chester, N.J. of the Diocese of Paterson was approved by Bishop Lawrence B. Casey on March 25, 1974, the feast of the Annunciation, and was founded by Rev. Eugene C.L. Romano on March 4, 1975.

Born of the faith, prayers and sacrifices of many friends and benefactors, to whose memory it is a living tribute, Bethlehem is nestled in a beautiful 18.5 acre parcel of peaceful and isolated woodland adjacent to 3,000 acres of the Black River Wildlife Reserve. There are twelve hermitages, a Chapel, Central House for the hermits, and St. Joseph's House for guests.

Hermit life as a Christian vocation had its earliest expression in the experience of Abraham, Moses, Elijah and St. John the Baptist, desert prophets who prepared for the Kingdom of God. The lives of these great religious figures were imitated in the third and fourth centuries by men and women like St. Anthony the Great who fled into the solitude of the deserts of Judea and Egypt so they might live the Christian life without compromise, thus forging the earliest foundation of a monastic life that took different forms over the centuries. Many were hermits who lived in a colony called a "Laura" and practiced obedience to a Desert Father or Mother.

In the recent Code of Canon Law of 1983, the Roman Catholic Church for the first time in history gave canonical recognition to the hermit vocation. This ancient tradition has been revived in the Diocese of Paterson through the canonical establishment of the Hermits of Bethlehem in the Heart of Jesus as a Public Association of the Christian Faithful (Catholic men and women) under the ecclesiastical authority of the local Bishop, Most Reverend Frank J. Rodimer. Bishop Rodimer gave final approval to the Rule of Life and Statutes on June 26, 1992, the Solemnity of the Sacred Heart of Jesus.

Desert Spirituality

The hermit of Bethlehem lives a life of contemplation in intimate union with God in response to His call to holiness and in greater separation from the world. It is a consecrated, solitary life of obedience, poverty and chastity lived in an unceasing prayer and joyful penance in the silence of solitude for the praise of God and the salvation of the world.

Nourished by exterior and interior silence, the hermit fulfills the purpose of his/her life and vocation by responding in solitude to a continual call to conversion heard in the heart and soul and leading to a life of faith, hope and love that puts one in touch with the reality of the false self and the truth of God. By living always in His presence and by daily offering and surrendering his/her life to God, the hermit seeks to grow in the perfection of love that mirrors the Heart of Jesus.

Although solitary, the hermit is not isolated or removed from the mainstream of life. Rather he/she is consecrated for the "salvation of the world" where people are isolated from each other and from God by hatred and sin. United with God and suffering humanity, the hermit is a whole person whose life is a deepening of "life hidden with Christ in God" (Col 3:2), thus furthering His Kingdom of love, justice and peace. The hermit of Bethlehem follows Jesus who invited us "to pray to our Father in secret" (Mt 6:5) and who "often retired to desert places and prayed" (Lk 5:16). The hermit stands before the Face of God to render Him service of loving and prayerful attentiveness.

The hermit's life of prayer is not only for his/her own personal sanctification but for the Church, its mission of evangelization and the whole human family. The hermit's spirituality flows from the infinite love of the Holy Trinity nourished by the daily Eucharistic Sacrifice of the Mass, the Gospel of Jesus Christ, Eucharistic Adoration, the Liturgy of the Hours and Lectio Divina. The hermit embraces the concerns of the Heart of Christ by making His prayer his/her own: "Our Father in heaven, hallowed be Your name, Your Kingdom come, Your will be done on earth as it is in heaven" (Mt 6:9-10); and Christ's prayer for unity: "that they may be one, as we are one" (Jn 17:22).

The hermits of Bethlehem together form a Laura living in separate solitary hermitages around a Chapel and Central House. Under the protection of Mary, Mother of the Incarnate Word and our mother, the hermit lives in obedience to the Desert Father who serves the brothers and sisters by guiding each one in the way of desert spirituality and discerning with each one the best way to live his/her particular life within the Laura according to Bethlehem's Rule of Living. The hermits support one another in solitude while exercising a life of mature, responsible freedom to adapt Bethlehem's Way of Living when necessary. This flexibility contrasts with monastic, cenobitical, cloistered living where most exercises are held in common.

Desert Hospitality

The guest at Bethlehem is welcomed into his/her own desert experience as though he/she were Christ Himself entering the peaceful, wooded surroundings that breathe a healing atmosphere of prayer created by the desert life of silence and solitude. Savoring this atmosphere becomes an effective passage to the presence of God and is preferred to a program of prayer.

The "desert" at Bethlehem is an oasis of healing and renewal for clergy, religious and lay men and women. Strengthened by solitude, silence and prayer, the guest leaves this sanctuary of peace like the first shepherds of Bethlehem, "glorifying and praising God" (Lk 2:20) and proclaiming His gospel of love, peace and joy.

VOCATIONAL CONTACT:

Rev. Eugene L. Romano, HBHJ
Desert Father
Bethlehem Hermitage, P.O. Box 315
82 Pleasant Hill Rd.
Chester, New Jersey 07930
Phone (908) 879-7059